COCKTAIL
GENIUS

COCKTAIL GENIUS

ALLAN GAGE

MQP

For Ella & Eddy

Published by **MQ Publications Limited**
12 The Ivories, 6–8 Northampton Street
London N1 2HY
TEL: 020 7359 2244
FAX: 020 7359 1616
EMAIL: mail@mqpublications.com
WEBSITE: www.mqpublications.com

Copyright © MQ Publications Limited 2004
Text © Allan Gage 2004

SERIES EDITOR: **abi rowsell**
DESIGN CONCEPT: **balley design associates**
LINE ILLUSTRATION: **karen hood**
GENIUS CARICATURE: **chris garbutt**

ISBN: 1-84072-541-9

1 3 5 7 9 0 8 6 4 2

Printed in China

This book contains the opinions and ideas of the author. It is intended to provide helpful and informative material on the subjects addressed in this book and is sold with the understanding that the author and publisher are not engaged in rendering any kind of personal professional services in this book. The author and publisher disclaim all responsibility for any liability, loss, or risk, personal or otherwise, which is incurred as a consequence, directly or indirectly, of the use and application of any of the contents of this book.

IMPORTANT Those who might be at risk from the effects of salmonella food poisoning (the elderly, pregnant women, young children, and those suffering from immune deficiency diseases) should consult their medical practitioner with any concerns about eating raw eggs.

Weights and Measurements

The recipes in this book are based on the measurements for one drink. However, ingredients are given in ratio form to make it easy to mix a greater number of cocktails.
For one drink, one "measure" corresponds to 1 fl oz US or 25 ml. You can use whatever type of measure you like; a pony holds 1 fl oz US, a jigger 1½ fl oz US.

Liquid ingredients:

bar spoon	$\frac{1}{16}$ fl oz	2 ml
dash	$\frac{1}{8}$ fl oz	5–10 ml
½ measure	½ fl oz	12.5 ml
1 measure	1 fl oz	25 ml
1½ measures	1½ fl oz	37.5 ml
2 measures	2 fl oz	50 ml

Dry ingredients:

	1 in	2.5 cm
	1 oz	25 g

introduction

Cocktails are once again enjoying their place at the cutting edge of cool. They became a symbol of bad taste throughout the 80s and early 90s, thanks to Tom Cruise's movie and the over-use of paper umbrellas. Screaming Orgasms, Sex on the Beach, Sloe Comfortable Screws—it became impossible to order a drink without going red in the face. Nowadays though, visit the "Style Bars" of one of the world's great cities—London, New York, Sydney, Barcelona to name a few—and it's clear from the drinking habits of the well-heeled clientele that once again cocktails are the epitomy of stylish excess.

The pages of this book are brimming with recipes and insider tips that will enable you to reproduce these delicious concoctions, and give you confidence next time you're in a bar to order exactly what you want. There is a cocktail for everyone in these pages to suit any mood, at anytime, anywhere.

What is it that makes a cocktail so enticing? Sure, they taste good. But there's a lot more to a cocktail than what goes into the glass. Cocktails have the ability to spark conversation and encourage romance, making every encounter intimate. It is the bartender's pleasure to pour a drink, serve it ... and then sit back and watch as his cocktail spins its magic. The seductive taste and look of a French Martini *(page 22)* for example, lends itself perfectly to a flirtatious, candle-lit conversation. The deliciously refreshing Apple-Soaked Mojito *(page 91)* is just made to be shared. If beer was created for men as compensation for the creation of women, and wine was created for women to make men a little more interesting, then cocktails might well be the chosen weapon of the modern-day Cupid.

And what of the cocktail drinker? History is littered with "great" drinkers, whose favorite tipples and resulting antics are well documented. Each of them brought their own unique touch to the art of the cocktail. Ernest Hemingway liked his Daiquiris mixed with Grapefruit Juice and Maraschino liqueur; Sarah Hubbard loves a dose of fresh lychee in her Martinis; Keith Richards' favourite Bourbon is Rebel Yell, mixed with ice and more Rebel Yell. As Frank Sinatra commented, "I feel sorry for people who don't drink, they wake up in the morning and that's as good as they're going to feel all day!"

The art of cocktail-making is to take the rules and then break them. There is no single way to mix drinks and every bar tender worth his tip has a secret recipe or a special ingredient which makes their Bloody Mary so special. I divulge my own "secret" recipe for the world's best known hangover-cure on page 17. The combination of fresh dill and Dijon mustard gives a subtle yet complex twist to this classic. My advice is: don't treat this book as a rule book. Use it to inspire you towards your own creative cocktail inventions.

So whether you're celebrating or relaxing make sure you grab a shaker, squeeze a grapefruit, raid the liquor cupboard, muddle a mint sprig, have a few too many, pulp a mango, juggle some bottles, juice anything you can find and generally just treat yourself—and others—to some liquid love.

Cheers,

A.G.

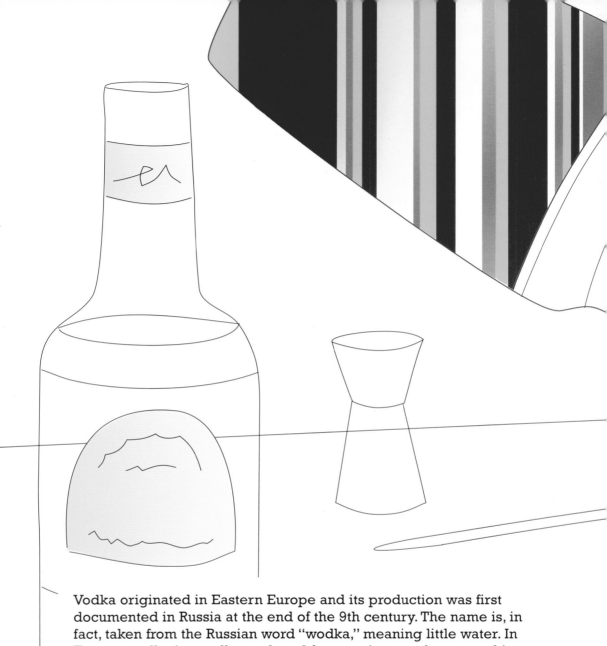

Vodka originated in Eastern Europe and its production was first documented in Russia at the end of the 9th century. The name is, in fact, taken from the Russian word "wodka," meaning little water. In Europe, vodka is usually produced from grain or molasses, and in Eastern Europe it is also produced from potatoes and rice. Vodka took a long time to gain popularity in the west and it was only in the 1960s and 70s that the drink started to become fashionable. Its versatility and mixability as a drink has made it a firm favorite in bars all over the world.

vodka

Caipiroska

1 lime, segmented | 1 dash sugar syrup
1 teaspoon brown sugar | 2 measures vodka

Muddle the sugar, lime segments, and sugar syrup in the bottom of an old-fashioned glass. Fill the glass with crushed ice, then add the vodka and stir. Serve with a stirrer and straw.

Get fruity Lime too sour for you? Then why don't you get fruity and make yourself a Caipiroska with a difference? Use your favorite fruit to replace half of the lime. To intensify the fruit flavor, you could replace the sugar syrup with a dash of fruit-flavored syrup or liqueur.

Screwdriver

2 measures vodka | orange slices, to garnish
freshly squeezed orange juice, to top

Pour the vodka into an ice-filled highball glass. Top with freshly squeezed orange juice and stir. Garnish with orange slices and serve with straws.

Cape Codder

2 measures vodka | 2 wedges of lime
4 measures cranberry juice |

Pour the vodka and cranberry juice into a highball glass over ice. Squeeze the lime wedges into the drink and drop in. Stir, and serve with straws.

Chi-Chi

1½ measures vodka | 1 dash freshly squeezed
2 measures pineapple juice | lime juice
1 measure coconut cream | 1 pineapple slice and 1 cocktail
(see page 76) | cherry, to garnish

Blend the vodka, pineapple juice, coconut cream, and lime juice with a scoop of crushed ice in a blender. Pour into a coupette (see below) or large champagne saucer and garnish with slice of pineapple and cherry.

Looking good Next time you're sipping margaritas by the pool, impress your friends and pour their drinks into a coupette. A what? This is the glass traditionally used to serve margaritas in. It has a wide saucer with a deep "pocket"—a little like a wide champagne saucer. And it's function? To look good!

Victory Collins

1½ measures Stolichnaya Vanil
(vanilla-flavored vodka)
½ measure freshly squeezed
lemon juice

1 bar spoon fine white sugar
2 measures grape juice
orange slices, to garnish

Fill a large highball glass with crushed ice. Shake the vodka, lemon juice, and sugar together (to dissolve) without ice. Pour this mixture over the crushed ice, add the grape juice, and stir. Garnish with slices of orange and serve with straws.

Shaken, not stirred Generally, the idea of shaking is to chill your drink and combine its flavors. So, shake hard and shake fast—shake too long and you'll dilute your concoction.

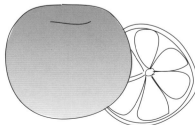

Cielo

1½ measures vodka
1 measure crème de cassis
(black currant liqueur)
2 dashes Peychaud's bitters
(anise-flavored bitter)

½ lime, juice only
ginger ale, to top
1 lime wedge, to garnish

Build all ingredients over ice in a highball glass, stir, and top with ginger ale. Garnish with a wedge of lime and serve with straws.

Ignorance

1 measure Ketel One Citroen
(lemon-flavored vodka)
½ measure Campari

½ measure passion fruit syrup
2 measures apple juice
1 orange twist, to garnish

Shake all the ingredients with ice and strain over ice into a large old-fashioned glass, or serve straight up, strained into a chilled martini glass. Garnish with an orange twist.

Cocktail lingo When you're ordering your drink, you need to know how to talk the talk. If you like lots of ice in an old-fashioned or high ball glass, then ask for it "on the rocks." But if you prefer it "martini style" with no ice cubes order it "straight up."

Black Russian

1½ measures vodka | Coca-Cola (optional)
1 measure Kahlua (coffee liqueur) |

Pour all of the ingredients over ice in an old-fashioned glass (use a highball, if using Coca-Cola) and stir.

The long and short of it This is a drink with a split personality! Without coca-cola, the Black Russian makes a strong, short drink with a punch. But add coca-cola and it's magically transformed into a long, refreshing summer drink.

White Russian

1½ measures vodka | 2 measures light cream
1 measure Kahlua (coffee liqueur) |

Pour the ingredients over ice in an old-fashioned glass, stir to mix and serve with short straws. To make this a little less rich, use half milk and half cream.

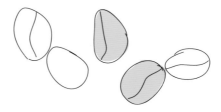

CranKiss

1 measure Finlandia Cranberry (cranberry-flavored vodka)
1 dash freshly squeezed lime juice
1 dash cranberry cordial

Champagne, to top
1 lime twist and cranberries, to garnish

Build all of the ingredients in a Champagne flute, stir, and garnish with the lime twist and cranberries.

Elderflower Fizz

1 measure Polstar Cucumber (cucumber-flavored vodka)
½ measure elderflower cordial

Champagne, to top
lemon peel
2 peeled cucumber slices

Pour all of the ingredients into a Champagne saucer. Wipe the rim of the glass with the lemon peel, stir, and garnish with the two slices of skinless cucumber.

Cool as a cucumber For subtle summer flavors, try adding cucumber to a bottle of vodka. Cut the cucumber into strips narrow enough to fit down the neck of your vodka bottle. (You might have to drink a bit of the vodka to make room for the cucumber!) Then re-seal the bottle and rotate every two days for two weeks. Filter the vodka through coffee filter paper and keep chilled. This is a great base for a Bloody Mary.

Bloody Mary (original)

2 measures vodka	4 dashes Worcestershire sauce
6 measures tomato juice	½ teaspoon cayenne pepper
1 dash freshly squeezed lemon juice	salt and pepper, to taste
	1 lime wedge, to garnish

Shake all of the ingredients (except the lime wedge) with ice and strain into a highball glass over ice. Add the wedge of lime and serve with a straw.

The X factor Any old hand will tell you that every bartender has his own, unique way of mixing a Bloody Mary. It's the X factor—that certain something that gives the Bloody Mary its kick. Experiment with your own proportions and ingredients to make your Bloody Mary special to you.

Bloody Caesar

2 measures vodka	1 teaspoon horseradish
4 dashes Worcestershire sauce	celery salt and freshly ground black pepper, to taste
2 dashes Tabasco sauce	1 stick of celery, to garnish
6 measures clamato juice	

Mix all of the ingredients in a shaker, add ice, and shake briefly to mix. Strain the mix into a highball glass over ice and garnish with a stick of celery.

Plasma

½ teaspoon Dijon mustard
1 teaspoon fresh dill, chopped
2 measures Wyborowa Pepper
(pepper-flavored vodka)
2 drops Tabasco sauce
4 drops Worcestershire sauce
½ lemon, juice only

celery salt and freshly ground
black pepper, to taste
4 measures tomato juice
2 6-inch strips of cucumber and
½ cherry tomato seasoned with
salt and pepper, to garnish

Muddle the mustard and dill together in the base of a shaker to form a paste, then add all of the other ingredients with some ice. Shake to mix then strain into a highball glass over ice. Garnish with strips of cucumber and half a seasoned cherry tomato.

Chop! Chop! When your bartender gets his knife out, don't be scared! He's just chopping up his ingredients to maximize their look and flavor. Except when he's using mint— that tastes best when it's used as whole leaves.

Cosmopolitan

1½ measures **Ketel One Citroen** | 1 dash freshly squeezed lime juice
(lemon-flavored vodka) | 1 measure cranberry juice
1 measure triple sec | 1 flamed orange twist, to garnish

Shake all of the liquid ingredients with ice and strain into a chilled martini glass. Flame the orange twist over the surface (see below) and drop this into the drink.

Light my fire We all like to show off now and then, and the flamed orange twist never fails to impress. Cut a small oval of peel from an orange, leaving a little pith intact. Pinch the oval skin-side out holding it over a flame. Squeeze it firmly so that the zest oil is released. The zest oil will then ignite to give you an impressive flame, with a fantastic aroma.

Mandrapolitan

1½ measures **Absolut Mandrin** | 1 dash freshly squeezed lime juice
(orange-flavored vodka) | 4 drops orange bitters
1 measure Cointreau | 1 lime twist, to garnish
1 measure cranberry juice |

Shake all of the ingredients with ice and strain into a chilled martini glass. Garnish with a lime twist.

Sea Breeze

2 measures vodka
4 measures cranberry juice

2 measures freshly squeezed
grapefruit juice
lime wedges, to garnish

Build all of the ingredients over ice in a highball glass, stir, and garnish with lime wedges. Serve with straws.

Bay Breeze

2 measures vodka
4 measures cranberry juice

2 measures pineapple juice
lime wedges, to garnish

Fill a highball glass with ice, then add the vodka, cranberry, and pineapple juice. Stir and garnish with wedges of lime.

Vodka Martini

½ **measure dry vermouth** | **2 green pitted olives, to garnish**
2 measures chilled vodka |

Fill a mixing glass with ice and add the vermouth. Stir the contents to coat the ice and pour off any liquid, leaving only the flavored ice. Add the vodka and stir to chill. Double strain the mix into a chilled martini glass and garnish with two olives on a cocktail stick.

How dry is dry? Before mixing a martini, always ask your guests' preference. As the saying goes, "children should never mix martinis, they always use too much vermouth."

Saketini

1 measure vodka
1½ measures sake
½ measure orange curaçao

4 drops orange bitters
2 peeled cucumber slices,
   to garnish

Add all of the liquid ingredients to a mixing glass and add ice. Stir until thoroughly chilled and double strain into a chilled martini glass. Garnish with two thin slices of peeled cucumber.

French Martini

2 measures vodka
½ measure Chambord (French black raspberry liqueur)

1 measure pineapple juice
1 plump raspberry, to garnish

Pour all of the liquid ingredients into a shaker and add ice. Shake vigorously and strain into a chilled martini glass. Allow to settle briefly, then float the raspberry in the centre of the surface foam.

Vesper

1½ measures vodka | ½ measure dry vermouth
1½ measures gin | 1 lemon twist, to garnish

Shake all of the ingredients with ice and double strain into a chilled martini glass. Garnish with a twist of lemon.

James Bond created this drink in the 1953 book Casino Royale by Ian Fleming. It is named for his femme fatale—Vesper Lynd—and Bond remarked "I never have more than one drink before dinner. But I do like that one to be large, very strong, very cold, and very well made. I hate small portions of anything, particularly when they taste bad."

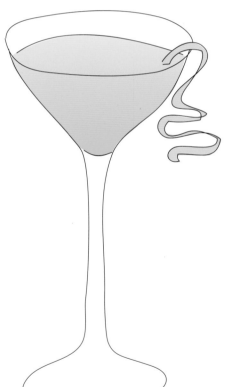

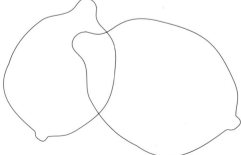

Polish Martini

1 measure Wyborowa Vodka (Polish vodka)
1 measure Zubrowka Bison Grass Vodka

1 measure krupnik vodka (honey-flavored vodka)
1 measure freshly pressed apple juice
1 lemon twist, to garnish

Stir all ingredients with ice to chill thoroughly and double strain into a chilled martini glass. Garnish with a twist of lemon.

Garden Martini

2 measures Polstar Cucumber (cucumber vodka)
8 mint leaves
1 dash sugar syrup

1 measure freshly pressed apple juice
1 lime wedge

Shake all of the ingredients with ice and double strain into a chilled martini glass. Squeeze the lime wedge over the drink and drop in as a garnish.

Mitch Martini

1½ measures Zubrowka Bison
Grass Vodka
½ measure passion fruit syrup
½ measure peach liqueur

1 measure freshly pressed
apple juice
1 lemon twist, to garnish

Shake all of the liquid
ingredients with ice and
double strain into a chilled
martini glass. Garnish with
a lemon twist.

Metrotini

4 blueberries
6 raspberries
2 measures krupnik vodka
(honey-flavored vodka)

½ measure Chambord (French
black raspberry liqueur)
1 measure freshly squeezed
lemon juice

Muddle the blueberries, plus four of the raspberries (reserving two
for a garnish) in the base of a shaker, add the liquid ingredients, and
shake with ice. Strain into a chilled martini glass and garnish with the
remaining two raspberries on a swizzle stick.

Tarte Tatin Martini

1½ measures Stolichnaya Vanil
(vanilla-flavored vodka)
1 dash orgeat syrup
(almond syrup)

½ measure apple schnapps
1 dash lemonade
whipped cream, to float
ground cinnamon, for dusting

Stir the vodka, syrup, and schnapps with ice to chill and strain into a chilled martini glass. Add the dash of lemonade and then float the cream on the surface. Dust the surface with ground cinnamon.

Light as a feather Want a cream float on top of your cocktail? No problem. Whip the cream so that it still has a liquid quality. Then stir the drink to create a whirlpool effect and pour the cream over a spoon which is in contact with the drink's surface. Nothing easier—except just drinking your wonderful concoction!

Watermelon Martini

4 chunks fresh watermelon
1 dash freshly squeezed lime juice
1 dash sugar syrup
2 measures Wyborowa Melon (melon-flavored vodka)

½ measure Passoã (passion fruit liqueur)
1 wedge of fresh watermelon, to garnish

In the base of a shaker, muddle the watermelon flesh, lime juice, and sugar syrup. Then add the vodka and Passoã. Fill with ice and shake vigorously. Double strain into a chilled martini glass and garnish with a lime twist.

Cocktail lingo It's not just the waiters who are smooth—your cocktail should be too. So to make sure your drink goes down well, bartenders do a "Double strain." This is a process by which bits of fruit and flecks of ice are removed from a drink by pouring the cocktail from the shaker through its strainer and then through a tea strainer.

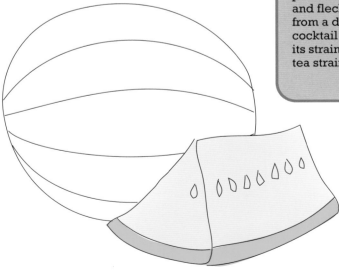

Zelda Martini

5 mint leaves
1 dash orgeat syrup (almond syrup)
2 measures Zubrowka Bison Grass Vodka

½ measure chilled water
1 measure freshly squeezed lime juice
1 mint sprig, to garnish

Bruise the mint leaves with the orgeat syrup in the base of a shaker. Add the vodka, water, and lime, then shake with ice. Double strain the mix into a chilled martini glass and garnish with the mint sprig.

The secret ingredient is…
Water! It's a little-known fact, but one of the most important ingredients for a good cocktail is good, old-fashioned water. You often need to dilute your cocktail to get exactly the right balance of taste and texture. This is usually achieved by shaking a cocktail with ice, but if you need to add it, use bottled water.

Martini Royale

2 measures frozen vodka
1 dash crème de cassis (black
currant liqueur)

Champagne, to top
1 lemon twist, to garnish

Pour the vodka and cassis into a
frozen martini glass and gently
stir. Top with chilled Champagne
and garnish with a twist of lemon.

Martini mania The martini
glass, sometimes simply called
a cocktail glass, has inspired
some great cocktail inventions.
Fruit-based, infused, creamy—
these "Neo-tinis" are all served
in the legendary martini glass.
But one word of caution: there is
nothing on earth more tragic
then a warm martini, so the
golden rules are: chill the glass
and drink swiftly.

Vochacino

1 measure vodka	½ teaspoon cocoa powder, plus a
½ measure Kahlua (coffee liqueur)	little extra for dusting
½ measure sugar syrup	1 measure light cream
½ measure cold espresso	

Shake all of the ingredients vigorously with ice and strain into a chilled martini glass. Garnish the surface by dusting with cocoa powder.

Twinkle

3 measures vodka	Champagne, to top
½ measure elderflower cordial	1 lemon twist, to garnish

Shake the vodka and elderflower cordial together and double strain into a large, chilled martini glass. Top with chilled Champagne, stir, and garnish with a lemon twist.

Fruit with a twist Bartenders don't use citrus twists just because they look pretty. These twists of fruit peel release the oils retained in the skin and impart just a hint of citrus flavor to the drink. To make a lemon twist, use a very sharp knife and slice an oval of citrus peel from the fruit. Scrape any white pith still attached to the twist and squeeze the twist over the drink surface before dropping it in.

Espresso Martini

1½ measures vodka | ½ measure Kahlua (coffee liqueur)
1 measure cold espresso | 1 dash sugar syrup

Shake all ingredients together
with ice and strain into a chilled
martini glass.

Kickstart your evening If you're feeling a bit out of sorts, go straight for
an Espresso Martini. This drink is probably the best pick-me-up available
in the modern cocktail bar. Trust me, you'll feel better for it!

Vanilla Haze

2 measures Stolichnaya Vanil | 1 measure freshly pressed
(vanilla-flavored vodka) | apple juice
½ measure passion fruit juice | 4 mint leaves
½ measure passion fruit syrup | 1 mint sprig, to garnish
2 drops orange bitters |

Shake all of the ingredients with
ice and double strain into a
chilled martini glass. Garnish
with the mint sprig.

cocktail genius

Apple Sip

2 measures Stolichnaya Vanil (vanilla-flavored vodka)
1 measure apple brandy
1 dash cinnamon syrup

1 measure freshly pressed apple juice
2 slices peeled apple, to garnish

Shake all of the liquid ingredients with ice and double strain into a chilled martini glass. Garnish with slices of peeled apple.

From Russia with Love

5 mint leaves
5 basil leaves
1 teaspoon sugar syrup

3 measures Stolichnaya Strasberi (strawberry-flavored vodka)
1 basil leaf and 1 split strawberry, to garnish

In the base of a shaker, bruise the mint and basil with the sugar syrup using a muddler. Add the vodka, fill with ice, and stir until chilled. Double strain the mix into a chilled martini glass and garnish with the split strawberry (see below) and basil leaf.

Strawberry split A tempting garnish is the split strawberry. Run a knife lengthways down the strawberry, leaving the stalk intact. Then press the fruit on to the rim of the glass, so that the strawberry sits open on the rim.

Blossom

½ **lime, juice only**
2 **measures Absolut Kurant**
(berry-flavored vodka)

½ **measure cold water**
1 **dash lime cordial**
1 **lime twist, to garnish**

Squeeze the lime into a shaker,
then add the other ingredients.
Shake with ice and double strain
into a chilled martini glass.
Garnish with a lime twist.

Chill out One of the most important ingredient for a good martini? A chilled glass. Either store it in the freezer or fridge, or fill with ice and soda water, and leave while preparing the cocktail. Just remember to empty the glass before straining the cocktail into it!

Road Runner

1½ **measures vodka**
1 **measure amaretto**
½ **measure coconut cream**
(see page 76)

1 **measure heavy cream**
ground nutmeg, for dusting

Shake all of the ingredients with ice and strain into a chilled martini glass. Dust the surface of the drink with ground nutmeg.

Moscow Mule

2 measures vodka | ginger ale, to top
½ lime, cut into wedges |

Add the vodka to an ice-filled highball glass, squeeze the lime wedges into the glass (drop into the drink once squeezed), stir, and top with ginger ale. Serve with straws.

Apple Blossom

1 measure vodka | 1 dash freshly squeezed
1 measure apple brandy | lemon juice
2 measures freshly pressed | 1 lemon twist, to garnish
apple juice |

Stir all of the ingredients with ice in a mixing glass. Strain over ice into an old-fashioned glass. Garnish with a lemon twist.

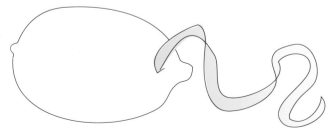

Harvey Wallbanger

2 measures vodka
4 measures freshly squeezed
orange juice

½ measure Galliano
1 orange slice, to garnish

Pour the vodka and orange juice into a large ice-filled highball glass and stir. Float some Galliano on top, garnish with an orange slice and serve with straws.

What's in a name? The Harvey Wallbanger is named after an Hawaiian surfer, Harvey, who having had his fill of vodka and oranges topped with Galliano, would stagger toward the door, crashing from wall-to-wall as he left. Many such dignified exits have since taken place thanks to the famous Harvey Wallbanger.

Holy Water

1½ measures vodka
½ measure triple sec
½ measure light rum

tonic water, to top
1 dash of grenadine
1 lemon, rind only, to garnish

Build the vodka, triple sec, and rum over ice in a large highball glass, stir, and charge with tonic water. Drizzle the grenadine through the drink before serving and garnish with the rind from a whole lemon.

Long Beach Iced Tea

½ measure vodka
½ measure gin
½ measure light rum
½ measure tequila

½ measure triple sec
1 dash freshly squeezed lime juice
cranberry juice, to top
lime wedges, to garnish

Add all of the alcoholic ingredients and lime juice to a shaker, add ice, and shake briefly. Strain into an ice-filled highball glass and top with cranberry juice. Stir, garnish with lime wedges, and serve with straws.

Lou's Iced Tea

2 measures Absolut Citron
(lemon-flavored vodka)
1 measure cranberry juice
½ measure freshly squeezed
orange juice

4 measures chilled Earl Grey tea
1 dash freshly squeezed
lemon juice
4 mint leaves
1 dash sugar syrup
lemon slices, to garnish

Shake all ingredients with ice and strain into a large ice-filled highball glass. Garnish with lemon slices and serve with straws.

Avalon

1½ measures vodka
½ measure Pisang Ambon (Dutch
banana-based liqueur)
2 measures freshly pressed
apple juice

1 dash freshly squeezed
lemon juice
lemonade, to top
red apple slices, to garnish

Fill a highball glass with ice.
Build the vodka, Pisang Ambon,
and apple and lemon juice in
the glass. Stir and top with
lemonade. Garnish with slices
of red apple.

Don't get browned off Lemon juice is one of the bartender's best
friends. Sliced fruit such as bananas and apples can quickly turn brown.
Prevent this by dousing the flesh in lemon juice, which also adds a
delicious citrus tang to the flavor.

'57 Chevy

1 measure vodka
1 measure Southern Comfort
½ measure Grand Marnier
2 measures pineapple juice

1 dash freshly squeezed
lemon juice
pineapple wedges, to garnish

Shake all of the ingredients with ice and strain into a highball glass
over ice. Garnish with pineapple wedges.

Rising Sun

2 measures vodka
2 measures freshly squeezed
grapefruit juice
½ measure passion fruit syrup
½ lemon, juice only
pink grapefruit slice, to garnish

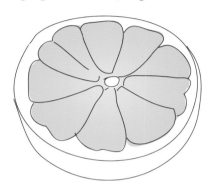

Shake all of the ingredients
together and strain over ice in
a large old-fashioned glass.
Garnish with a slice of pink
grapefruit and serve with straws

Bison's Plums

2 measures Zubrowka Bison
Grass Vodka
2 measures freshly pressed
apple juice
1 measure Mirabelle plum purée
1 dash freshly squeezed
lemon juice
lemon slices, to garnish

Shake all of the ingredients
together and strain over ice into
a slim highball glass. Garnish
with lemon slices and serve
with straws.

The queen of fruits Wondering what all the fuss is about? Well, the
Mirabelle plum is an unusual golden-colored plum originating from Asia,
and it is valued for its superbly subtle flavor. Try it—it's something special!

Rapaska

2 measures Stolichnaya Razberi
(raspberry-flavored vodka)
1 measure passion fruit purée
1 measure raspberry purée
½ passion fruit

1 measure freshly pressed
apple juice
1 measure freshly squeezed
orange juice
2 raspberries and 1 apple wedge,
to garnish

Shake all of the ingredients briefly with crushed ice and transfer to a highball glass. Do not strain. Garnish with raspberries and an apple wedge, and serve with straws.

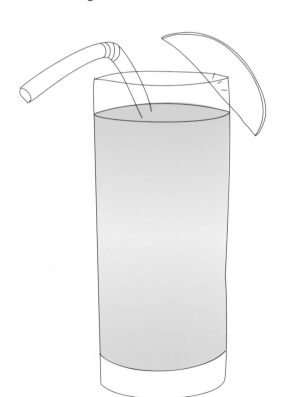

Juicy fruity Some of the best homemade drinks don't involve alcohol at all. Fruit purées can be easily made by chopping fruit into small pieces and blending (without ice) on high speed. You may want to adjust the sweetness of a purée using sugar syrup. Some great examples of easily produced purées are mango, strawberry, raspberry, and plum. Refreshing, and healthy too!

Kinky Mole

2 measures Absolut Kurant (berry-flavored vodka)
1 dash orgeat syrup (almond syrup)

2 measures freshly squeezed pink grapefruit juice
2 dashes crème de mure (blackberry liqueur)
2 blackberries, to garnish

Shake all of the liquid ingredients and strain over ice into a large highball glass. Garnish with blackberries and serve with straws.

Miss Scarlett

8 fresh raspberries
½ lime, cut into wedges
1 dash sugar syrup

2 measures Stolichnaya Razberi (raspberry-flavored vodka)
soda water, to top.

In the base of a highball glass, muddle the raspberries, lime, and sugar syrup. Fill the glass with ice, and add the vodka. Transfer the contents of the glass into a shaker and shake. Then pour back into the highball glass. Do not strain. Top with soda water, stir, and serve with straws.

Honey Berry Sour

1½ measures krupnik vodka (honey-flavored vodka)
½ measure Chambord (French black raspberry liqueur)

1 measure freshly squeezed lemon juice
1 dash sugar syrup
2 raspberries, to garnish

Shake all of the liquid ingredients with ice and strain over ice into a large old-fashioned glass. Garnish with two raspberries and serve with straws.

> **Insider tricks** Watch your bartender next time he's preparing to squeeze some citrus juice into your drink. If he rolls the fruit around on the bar, he hasn't lost his mind. This allows him to extract the maximum amount of juice from the fruit. Clever, huh?

Fresca

1 small pink grapefruit, segmented
1 teaspoon brown sugar

2 measures vodka
lemonade, to top

Muddle the grapefruit and sugar in the base of a boston glass until sugar is dissolved, then fill the glass with ice. Add vodka and stir, then top with lemonade. Stir again and serve with a stirrer and straws.

Passion Charge

1 passion fruit	1½ measures Absolut Mandrin
1 dash freshly squeezed lime juice	(orange-flavored vodka)
1 dash passion fruit syrup	Red Bull (energy drink), to top
2 measures cranberry juice	lime wedges, to garnish

Spoon the flesh of the passion fruit into the base of a highball glass. Add lime juice, syrup, cranberry juice, and vodka. Fill the highball glass with ice, transfer to a shaker, shake, and return to the glass, unstrained. Top with Red Bull, stir, and garnish with lime wedges. Serve with straws.

Kumquat May

5 kumquats, chopped	1½ measures Absolut Vanilla
1 dash cinnamon syrup	(vanilla-flavored vodka)
½ measure kiwi schnapps	

Briefly muddle the chopped kumquats with the cinnamon syrup in the base of a shaker. Then add all the other ingredients, shake with ice, and transfer to a large old-fashioned glass, unstrained. Serve with straws.

Madras

2 measures vodka
4 measures cranberry juice
2 measures freshly squeezed
orange juice

orange slices, to garnish

Build all of the ingredients over ice in a highball glass, stir, and garnish with orange slices. Serve with straws.

Fun to share Like most things in life, cocktails always taste better when you share them with someone. The Madras and the Sea Breeze (see page 19) are perfect examples of tasty cocktails that serve groups of people well—simple, refreshing, and easy to make. Fill a pitcher with ice, build the ingredients, stir, and pour.

Kitsch Revolt

1 measure Absolut Kurant
(berry-flavored vodka)
½ measure strawberry purée

Champagne, to top
strawberry slices, to garnish

Shake the vodka and strawberry purée together briefly with ice and strain into a chilled flute. Top with Champagne, stir, and garnish with slices of strawberry.

Russian Spring Punch

1 measure Stolichnaya Vodka (Russian vodka)
1 measure freshly squeezed lemon juice
½ measure raspberry purée
½ measure créme de cassis (black currant liqueur)

1 dash framboise (raspberry liqueur)
1 dash sugar syrup
champagne, to top
2 lemon slices and raspberries, to garnish

Shake all ingredients except champagne with ice and strain over crushed ice into a sling glass. Top with champagne, stir, and garnish with two lemon slices and fresh raspberries.

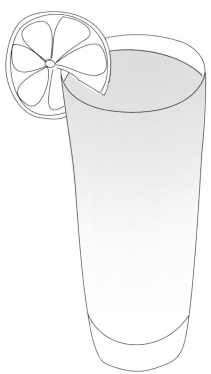

In the beginning… Vodka came from Russia. Or maybe Poland. It's a subject of heated debate, and no one really knows who was the first barman to pour a shot of vodka! Vodka translates in Russian as "little water," and definitely stems as far back as the 9th century. But vodka as we know it today only really appeared in the 18th century, when it became possible to purify spirits by filtration.

Buck's Twizz

1 peeled pink grapefruit slice
1 measure Absolut Mandrin
(orange-flavored vodka)

1 measure freshly squeezed
orange juice
½ measure maraschino liqueur
Champagne, to top

Place the slice of pink grapefruit in the bottom of a large Champagne saucer. Briefly shake the vodka, orange juice, and liqueur with ice and strain over the grapefruit. Top with Champagne, and stir.

Pot Shot

1 lime wedge
1 measure Absolut Kurant
(berry-flavored vodka)

1 dash peach schnapps

Squeeze the lime wedge into a shaker; add the vodka and schnapps, then shake briefly with ice. Strain into a chilled shot glass, and drink it in one gulp.

Oyster Shot

1 small plump oyster
3 drops Tabasco sauce
2 drops Worcestershire sauce
pinch salt
pinch black pepper

1 squeezed lemon wedge
½ measure chilled Absolut Peppar
(pepper-flavored vodka)
½ measure tomato juice

In a shot glass, build the ingredients in the exact order detailed above, starting with the oyster. Stir the shot briefly and let it slip down in one.

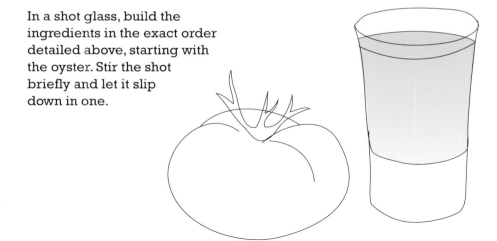

Swizzle

1 dash passion fruit syrup | **1 measure Grey Goose L'orange**
1 dash Campari | **(quality orange-flavored vodka)**

Layer the ingredients in
the following order: syrup,
Campari, vodka.

Flying high It's not grey, and there are no geese involved—but it does
taste of oranges. Grey Goose L'orange is an orange-flavored vodka
originating from the Cognac Region of France. Clear mineral water is
infused with an essence of orange. Then a five-step distillation process
creates the crisp, citrus flavor of fresh oranges that is enjoyed around
the world. Salut!

Body Shot

1 teaspoon white sugar | **1 lemon wedge**
1 measure chilled vodka |

Using a partner, lick their neck to moisten. Pour the sugar onto their
neck in the moistened area. Place wedge of lemon in their mouth
with the skin pointed inward. You must first lick the sugar from their
neck, then the vodka, then suck the lemon from their mouth.
What an ice-breaker!

Pink Sin

1 teaspoon fine white sugar
1 dash red food coloring
1 measure chilled Absolut
Mandrin (orange-flavored vodka)

1 dash framboise (raspberry
  liqueur)
1 lime wedge coated, to garnish

Mix a spoonful of fine white sugar with a drop of red food coloring, to create pink sugar and use it to coat the lime wedge. Add the chilled vodka and liqueur to a shot glass, stirring to mix. Serve with the lime wedge coated in pink sugar.

383

¼ measure Frangelico
1 measure chilled Stolichnaya
  Razberi (raspberry-
  flavored vodka)

orange wedge dusted with brown
  sugar, to garnish

Pour the Frangelico and then the chilled vodka into a shot glass. Down this in one mouthful and follow it with a bite of the sugared orange.

Bloody Simple

1 ripe tomato wedge
celery salt and freshly ground
black pepper, to taste

1 measure chilled Absolut Peppar
(pepper-flavored vodka)
2 drops Tabasco sauce

Season a wedge of ripe tomato
with celery salt and pepper.
Pour the chilled vodka into a
shot glass and add two drops of
Tabasco. Serve with the tomato.

Raff Slammer

1 measure vodka | 1 measure bitter lemon

Add all of the ingredients to an
old-fashioned glass. Cover the
glass with your hand, slam firmly
three times against a hard, stable
surface, and down the drink in
one while it is still fizzing.

Kamikaze

1 measure vodka
½ measure Cointreau

2 dashes freshly squeezed
lemon juice

Shake all of the ingredients very briefly with ice and strain into a shot glass. This shot is best made in larger quantities, so either share some or have a few. Add a dash of Chambord before drinking and this becomes a Purple Haze.

All shook up If you're shaking for one, you may as well shake for two. With shaken shots, it is always best to make them for at least two people. This is because with the ingredients and the dilution from shaking, there will be more than a single shot to serve. And don't forget, it's always far more fun to share.

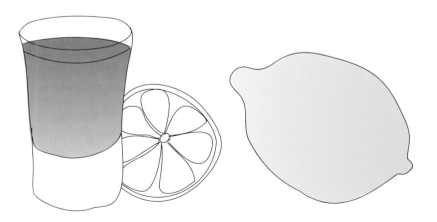

Originally used for medicinal purposes, it is thought that gin was first produced in Holland in the 17th century. It was in the 1920s, "the Cocktail Age," that gin began to be drunk by high society, most commonly enjoyed with tonic and a wedge of lime, or in a martini. It is widely regarded as one of the most essential beverages to stock for those entertaining at home. The name "gin" was taken from the French word for juniper, "genievre," as juniper is one of many flavors that is added to the spirit.

chapter **2**

gin

Martini Thyme

1 bunch of lemon thyme, stalks removed
1 dash sugar syrup

1½ measures gin
1 measure Green Chartreuse (herb liqueur)
3 olives, to garnish

Reserve a lemon thyme leaf to use as a garnish. Muddle the rest of the thyme with the sugar syrup in the base of a shaker. Add remaining ingredients, shake with ice, and double strain into a chilled martini glass. Garnish with three olives and the reserved lemon thyme leaf on a swizzle stick.

In a muddle Herbs aren't just for cooking—they're for drinking, too! But whenever you use herbs in a cocktail, always treat them with respect. Remove the stalks, especially when muddling the herb (such as mint in a Mojito). Otherwise, the stalks will give an unpleasant, bitter aftertaste to the drink.

Paradise Martini

2 measures gin
1½ measures freshly squeezed orange juice

½ measure apricot brandy
4 drops orange bitters
1 flamed orange twist (see page 18)

Shake all of the ingredients with ice and then double strain into a chilled martini glass. Flame the orange twist over the drink's surface and drop it in.

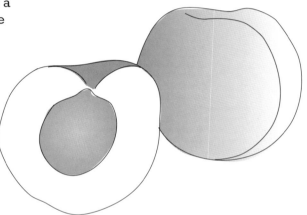

Lady Martini

1½ measures gin
½ measure apple brandy
½ measure freshly squeezed lemon juice

1 dash orgeat syrup (almond syrup)
½ egg white (see page 69)

Shake all of the ingredients with ice and strain into a chilled martini glass.

Mayflower Martini

1½ measures gin	1 dash elderflower cordial
½ measure apricot brandy	½ measure freshly squeezed
1 measure freshly pressed	lemon juice
apple juice	1 edible flower petal, to garnish

Shake all of the ingredients with ice and double strain into a chilled martini glass. Float the petal on the drinks surface as a garnish.

Jazzing up Juniper Who would have thought that the humble Juniper berry could be responsible for so much merriment? In fact, gin was first made from the seeds of a juniper berry for its medicinal properties until it became a drink of fashion in 18th-century England.

Raspberry Martini

8 raspberries	½ measure framboise (raspberry
1 dash sugar syrup	liqueur)
1 measure sloe gin	2 raspberries, to garnish
1 measure gin	

Muddle the raspberries and sugar syrup in the base of a shaker, then add all the other ingredients and shake vigorously with ice. Double strain into a chilled martini glass and float two raspberries on the surface.

Aviation

1½ measures gin	1 measure freshly squeezed
2 dashes maraschino cherry	lemon juice
liqueur	1 cocktail cherry, to garnish

Shake first three ingredients with ice and strain into a chilled martini glass. Garnish with a single cocktail cherry.

Blue Bird

3 measures gin	4 drops Angostura bitters
1 measure triple sec	1 lemon twist, to garnish

Shake the first three ingredients with ice and strain into a chilled martini glass. Garnish with a lemon twist.

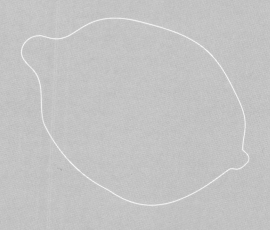

Breakfast Martini

1 teaspoon orange marmalade
2 measures gin
1 dash freshly squeezed
lemon juice

½ measure triple sec
1 small triangle of toast spread
with butter and marmalade

Stir the marmalade with the gin in a shaker until dissolved, then add the lemon juice and triple sec. Shake until thoroughly chilled. Strain into a chilled martini glass and garnish with the toast slice.

Dry Martini

½ measure Noilly Prat (dry
vermouth)

2 measures gin
1 olive or 1 lemon twist, to garnish

Stir the vermouth with ice in a mixing glass then strain away any excess liquid so that just the coated ice remains. Add the gin and stir until chilled. Strain the mix into a chilled martini glass and garnish with a lemon twist or olive on a cocktail stick.

What's in a name? Noilly Prat is well-known as one of the finest dry vermouths available. Made from wine and stored in Canadian oak, a complex process using fortification and the addition of various herbs produces this very fresh and complex aperitif.

Wibble

1 measure sloe gin
1 measure gin
1 measure freshly squeezed grapefruit juice
1 dash freshly squeezed lemon juice

1 dash sugar syrup
1 dash crème de mure (blackberry liqueur)
1 lemon twist

Shake all the ingredients with ice and strain into a chilled martini glass. Squeeze the oils from the lemon twist over the drink's surface and drop in as a garnish.

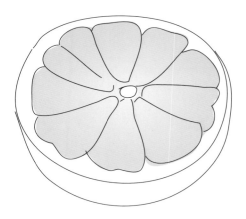

Gibson Martini

½ measure extra dry vermouth
2 measures gin

4 pearl onions

Stir the vermouth with ice in a mixing glass then strain away any excess liquid so just the coated ice remains. Add the gin and stir until thoroughly chilled. Strain the mix into a chilled martini glass and garnish with the onions on a swizzle stick. Garnished with an olive or lemon twist instead this will become a Dry Martini (see opposite).

Opal Martini

2 measures gin
1 measure triple sec or Cointreau
2 measures freshly squeezed
orange juice

1 flamed orange twist
(see page 18)

Shake all of the ingredients with ice and strain into a chilled martini glass. Garnish with a flamed orange twist.

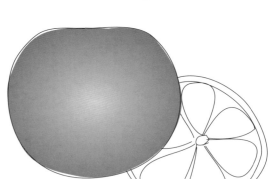

Speak-easy sensations
If there's one good thing to come out of the American Prohibition, it is the Opal Martini. Widely regarded as the original "Neo-tini," this drink was originally designed to mask the flavor of ropey tasting gin. It remains a wonderfully balanced—and very potent—drink, despite its insalubrious beginnings.

Gimlet

2 measures gin
1 measure lime cordial

½ measure water (optional)
1 lime wedge

Stir all of the liquid ingredients with ice until thoroughly chilled and strain into a chilled martini glass. Squeeze the lime wedge over the drink and drop in.

Maxim

1½ measures gin
1 measure dry vermouth

1 dash white crème de cacao
(chocolate-flavored liqueur)
1 cocktail cherry

Shake all of the ingredients with ice until thoroughly chilled, then strain into a chilled martini glass. Garnish with a cocktail cherry.

 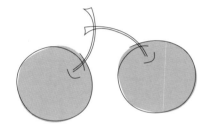

Paisley Martini

1½ measures gin
½ measure extra dry vermouth

2 dashes Scotch whisky
1 lemon twist, to garnish

Shake all of the liquid ingredients with ice and strain into a chilled martini glass. Garnish with a lemon twist.

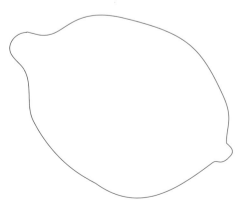

Park Avenue

1½ measures gin | 1 dash pineapple juice
1 measure sweet vermouth |

Stir all of the ingredients in a mixing glass with ice until thoroughly chilled. Strain into a chilled martini glass and serve immediately.

Alexander's Sister

1½ measures gin | 1 measure light cream
1 measure green crème de menthe | grated nutmeg, to garnish

Shake all of the liquid ingredients with ice and strain into a chilled martini glass. Finish with a sprinkle of grated nutmeg.

Take the taste test If you can taste the difference between the two crème de menthes—green and white—then you might need to refresh your taste buds. The two different colours exist for purely aesthetic reasons and both versions taste exactly the same.

Invitation Only

3 measures gin | 1 egg white (see page 69)
½ measure sugar syrup | 1 dash crème de mure
½ measure freshly squeezed | (blackberry liqueur)
lime juice | 2 blackberries, to garnish

Shake and strain the first four ingredients over ice into a
highball glass. Lace the drink with crème de mure and garnish
with two blackberries.

  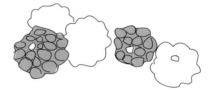

Arizona Cooler

4 measures cranberry juice | 2 measures grapefruit juice
2 measures gin | lime wedges, to garnish

Fill a highball glass with ice and add the cranberry juice. Shake
the gin and grapefruit juice with ice and strain over the cranberry
juice to create a "floating" effect. Garnish with lime wedges and
serve with straws.

Tom Collins

2 measures gin
1 measure freshly squeezed lemon juice

½ measure sugar syrup
soda water, to top
1 lemon slice, to garnish

Shake the first three ingredients with ice and strain into an ice-filled highball glass. Top with soda and stir gently. Garnish with a lemon slice and serve with straws.

Hedgerow Sling

2 measures sloe gin
1 measure freshly squeezed lemon juice
1 dash sugar syrup
soda water, to top

½ measure crème de mure (blackberry liqueur)
3 blueberries, 3 blackberries and 1 lemon slice, to garnish

Shake the gin, lemon juice, and sugar syrup with ice, and strain into an ice-filled highball glass. Top with soda water and lace with the crème de mure. Garnish with blueberries, blackberries, and a lemon slice.

Live a little Don't ignore those liqueurs hanging around at the back of your drinks cupboard. Crème de mure is a French blackberry liqueur which works fantastically well with the flavor of gin. Give it a go!

Sloe-Ho

1 measure sloe gin
1 measure gin
½ measure Chambord (black raspberry liqueur)
1 dash freshly squeezed lemon juice

1 dash sugar syrup
½ egg white (see page 69)
soda water, to top
1 lemon twist, to garnish

Shake the first six ingredients with ice and strain into an ice-filled highball glass. Top with soda water. Garnish with a lemon twist and serve with straws.

Royal raspberries Chambord is a French liqueur made from honey and black raspberries. The raspberries are hand-picked and then mellowed in oak barrels. The distinctive and royal-looking orb-shaped bottle with its brass decoration is a must-have in any cocktail bar.

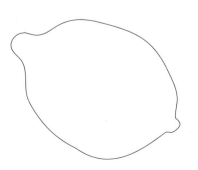

Bronx

2 measures gin
½ measure extra dry vermouth
½ measure sweet vermouth

1½ measures blood orange juice
1 cocktail cherry, to garnish

Shake all of the liquid ingredients with ice and strain into an old-fashioned glass over crushed ice. Garnish with a cocktail cherry and serve with short straws.

Ginger Tom

2 measures gin
1 measure ginger syrup
1 measure freshly squeezed lime juice

1 dash sugar syrup
sparkling mineral water, to top
1 lime wedge and 1 mint sprig, to garnish

Fill a highball glass with ice and add the gin, ginger syrup, lime juice, and sugar syrup. Stir gently to mix, then top with sparkling mineral water. Garnish with a squeeze of lime and a mint sprig.

Confused yet? There are three main styles of gin. London Dry Gin, which, despite its name, can be made anywhere in the world. Plymouth Gin, which can only be made in Plymouth, England because of the soft water available in the region. And Old Tom Gin, a sweet style, which was once the most popular but is now almost obsolete.

Arthur Tompkins

2 measures gin
½ measure Grand Marnier

1 dash freshly squeezed
lemon juice
1 lemon twist, to garnish

Shake the gin, Grand Marnier, and lemon juice briefly with ice and strain into an old-fashioned glass over ice. Garnish with a twist of lemon and serve with short straws.

Gin Sour

2 measures gin
2 measures freshly squeezed
orange juice
1 measure freshly squeezed
lemon juice

1 measure egg white (see page 69)
½ measure sugar syrup
1 lemon wedge, to garnish

Shake all of the liquid ingredients with ice and strain into an ice-filled highball glass. Garnish with a lemon wedge and serve with straws.

Greenback

1½ measures gin
1 measure green crème de menthe

1 measure freshly squeezed
lemon juice
lemon slices, to garnish

Shake all of the ingredients
briefly with ice and strain into an
old-fashioned glass over ice.
Garnish with lemon slices and
serve with short straws.

Tight squeeze Be gentle with your fruit! If you squeeze a lemon or lime
too hard the pith provides a very bitter flavor. Make that mistake, and you
may never be asked to mix a cocktail again.

Gin Geenie

6 mint leaves
½ measure freshly squeezed
lemon juice

1 dash sugar syrup
2 measures gin
1 mint sprig, to garnish

Muddle the mint leaves, lemon juice, and sugar syrup in the bottom of
an old-fashioned glass. Fill with crushed ice and stir. Slowly add the
gin and stir again. Garnish with a sprig of mint and serve with straws.

Bumble Bee

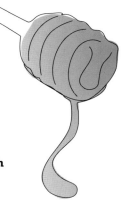

1 teaspoon liquid honey | 2 measures gin
1 dash freshly squeezed | 2 lemon slices, to garnish
lemon juice |

Fill an old-fashioned glass with crushed ice and add honey and lemon juice. Stir while slowly adding gin and top with more crushed ice. Garnish with lemon slices and serve with short straws.

Bramble

2 measures gin | ½ measure crème de mure
1½ measures freshly squeezed | (blackberry liqueur)
lemon juice | 1 blackberry and 1 lemon slice,
½ measure sugar syrup | to garnish

Fill an old-fashioned glass with crushed ice, add the first three ingredients, and stir. Top glass with more crushed ice then lace with crème de mure. Garnish with a blackberry and lemon slice and serve with two short straws.

Ice types Cubed, crushed, or shaved—the usage of each depends on the dilution required. The Bramble is a perfect example of a cocktail which benefits from the gradual dilution as the crushed ice melts.

Sweet Geenie

6 mint leaves | 1½ measures gin
½ measure freshly squeezed | ½ measure amaretto
lemon juice | 1 mint sprig, to garnish
1 dash sugar syrup |

Muddle the mint leaves, lemon juice, and sugar syrup in the bottom of an old-fashioned glass. Fill with crushed ice and stir. Slowly add the gin and stir again. Top with amaretto and garnish with a mint sprig. Serve with short straws.

French 75

1 measure gin | 1 dash sugar syrup
½ measure freshly squeezed | Champagne, to top
lemon juice | 1 lemon twist, to garnish

Shake the gin, lemon juice, and sugar syrup with ice and strain into a Champagne flute. Top with the Champagne, stir, and garnish with a lemon twist.

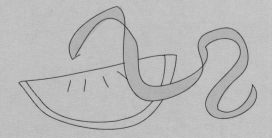

Sloe Gin Fizz

1 measure sloe gin
1 measure gin
1 measure freshly squeezed lime juice

1 dash sugar syrup
½ egg white (see below)
soda water, to top
lemon slices, to garnish

Shake the sloe gin, gin, lime juice, sugar syrup, and egg white with ice, and strain over ice into an old-fashioned glass. Top with soda water, stir, and garnish with slices of lemon.

Raw ingredients What's the oddest cocktail ingredient? Well, how about a raw egg white? It's an essential part of the Sloe Gin Fizz, but if the thought turns your stomach rather than wets your appetite you could always use pasteurized liquid egg white now available in supermarkets.

Maiden's Blush

1½ measures gin
½ measure triple sec
1 dash grenadine

1 dash freshly squeezed lemon juice
lemon slices, to garnish

Shake all of the liquid ingredients with ice and strain into an ice-filled old-fashioned glass. Garnish with lemon slices and serve with short straws.

Singapore Sling

2 measures gin
1 measure freshly squeezed orange juice
1 measure freshly squeezed lime juice
1 dash lime cordial
3 drops Angostura bitters

2 dashes Cherry Heering (cherry liqueur)
soda water, to top
1 dash Benedictine (brandy liqueur)
1 split lemon slice and 1 cherry, to garnish

Shake the gin, orange juice, lime juice, lime cordial, bitters, and 1 dash of the cherry liqueur with ice and strain into an ice-filled sling glass. Top with soda water and slowly add the remaining cherry liqueur and Benedictine so they float at the top of the glass. Garnish with a split lemon slice and a cherry, and serve with straws.

Take the vow Benedictine is one of the oldest liqueurs in the world, and is made up of a mysterious mix of 27 different herbs, plants, and peels.

Palm Beach

1 measure gin
½ measure extra dry vermouth
1 measure grapefruit juice

1 dash sugar syrup
1 pink grapefruit wedge, to garnish

Shake all of the ingredients with ice and strain into an ice-filled highball glass. Garnish with a pink grapefruit wedge and serve with straws.

cocktail genius

Raspberry Collins

2 measures gin
1½ measures raspberry purée
½ measure freshly squeezed
lemon juice
½ measure crème de framboise
(raspberry liqueur)

1 dash sugar syrup
1 dash orange bitters
soda water, to top
2 raspberries and 1 lemon slice,
to garnish

Shake first six ingredients with ice and strain into a highball glass filled with crushed ice. Top with soda water and stir. Garnish with raspberries and a lemon slice, serve with straws.

Mash it up There's nothing more satisfying, or healthy, than making your own puree from fresh fruit. But don't be too keen to drink it straight away. It may be necessary to strain your puree before use, especially when making raspberry purée. There are huge amounts of tiny seeds in the fruit, which taste gritty if left in. Run the purée through a fine sieve first.

Shady Grove Cooler

2 measures gin
1 measure freshly squeezed
lime juice

½ measure sugar syrup
ginger ale, to top
lime wedges, to garnish

Shake the gin, lime juice, and sugar syrup with ice and strain into an ice-filled highball glass. Top with ginger ale and stir. Garnish with lime wedges and serve with straws.

Orlando

1½ measures gin
2 dashes Chambord (black
raspberry liqueur)

2 measures pineapple juice
2 raspberries, to garnish

Shake the gin, Chambord, and pineapple juice vigorously (to create a surface foam) and strain into an ice-filled old-fashioned glass. Garnish with raspberries and serve with short straws.

Negroni

1 measure gin
1 measure Campari
1 measure sweet vermouth

soda water (optional), to top
½ orange slice, to garnish

Stir the gin, Campari, and vermouth in a mixing glass with ice and strain into an ice-filled highball glass. Top with soda and garnish with half an orange slice. Serve with short straws and a stirrer.

What's in a name? Take out the gin, and this becomes an Americano—the original form of the cocktail. An American GI, Mr. Negroni, wanted more of a kick in his drink while in an Italian bar during World War II, so the bartender added a shot of gin—and the Negroni was born.

Orange Buck

1½ measures gin
1 measure freshly squeezed orange juice

1 dash freshly squeezed lime juice
ginger ale, to top
lime wedges, to garnish

Shake all of the ingredients with ice and strain into an ice-filled highball glass. Top with the ginger ale and stir. Garnish with lime wedges and serve with straws.

Rum is said to date back to the early 16th century. At first it was a rough spirit that colonists drank, but its popularity later spread to Western Europe and then throughout the rest of the world. Rum is made from the sweet juice of sugar cane, however, some distilleries use molasses instead. In the present day, it is most common for all rum to be aged in used oak barrels from anywhere between one to thirty years. There are two types of rum, light and dark, the latter being a result of longer aging and the addition of caramel. Taste the sunshine of the Caribbean and lace your cocktails with rum!

rum

Piña Colada

1 measure white rum
1 measure Malibu (coconut rum)
1 measure coconut cream
(see below)

2 measures pineapple juice
4 chunks fresh pineapple
1 pineapple leaf and wedge,
to garnish

Blend all of these ingredients with one scoop of crushed ice in a blender at high speed. Serve with straws in a hurricane glass garnished with a pineapple leaf and wedge.

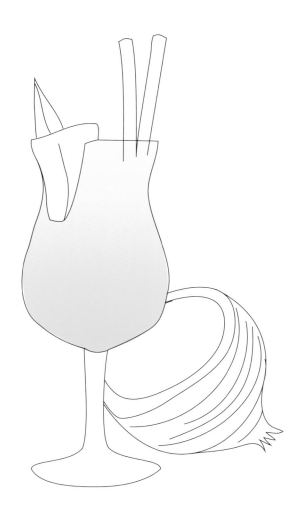

Crack open a coconut!
Don't let your coconuts confuse you. Most of us have heard of coconut milk, but it's actually coconut cream that's crucial to a good Piña Colada. It usually comes in tins and has a relatively short shelf life, so make sure you keep it refrigerated and use it quickly.

Hot Rum Punch

1 cup red grape juice
4 tablespoons brown sugar
1½ cups dark rum

6 cups dry white wine
2 cups red wine

This drink is to be made for a large group. In a large saucepan, warm the grape juice over a medium heat, then add the sugar, and stir until dissolved. Stir in the rum and both wines and continue to stir. Heat the mixture but do not boil. Serve hot, in wine goblets.

Planter's Punch

2 measures dark rum
2 measures freshly squeezed orange juice
1 dash grenadine

1 dash freshly squeezed lemon juice
lemon slices, to garnish

Shake all ingredients with ice and strain into an ice-filled old-fashioned glass. Garnish with lemon slices and serve with a stirrer.

Chetta's Punch

2 measures dark rum
1 measure undiluted black currant cordial
½ measure Cointreau
½ measure freshly squeezed lemon juice
4 drops orange bitters
1 orange slice, to garnish

Build all of the ingredients over ice in a heavy-based, old-fashioned glass. Stir to chill, garnish with an orange slice, and serve with a stirrer.

Cuban Breeze

3 measures cranberry juice
2 measures gold rum
2 measures freshly squeezed grapefruit juice
lime wedges, to garnish

Fill a highball glass with ice and add the cranberry juice. Shake the rum and grapefruit juice together with ice, and then strain over the cranberry juice, creating a "floating" effect. Garnish with lime wedges.

Rum deal There's a taste of the West Indies in every sip of rum thanks to one thing—molasses. Nearly all rum is made from this dark, sweet syrup which is a bi-product of sugar cane. Water is added and a special yeast joins the mix to aid fermentation. Then each rum distillery will add its own unique flavorings according to its closely-guarded recipe.

West Indian Iced Tea

1 measure Bacardi Oro
(gold rum)
½ measure Grand Marnier
1 measure freshly squeezed
orange juice

4 mint leaves
4 measures freshly brewed
English Breakfast tea
1 orange slice and 1 mint sprig,
to garnish

Shake all of the ingredients (including mint leaves—not sprig) with ice, and strain into an ice-filled highball glass. Garnish with an orange slice and mint sprig, and serve with straws, in the sun.

Canchanchara

1 measure liquid honey
2 measures white rum
1 measure freshly squeezed
lime juice

1 dash soda water
1 lime wedge, to garnish

In a heavy-based old-fashioned glass, stir the honey, rum, and lime juice until the honey has dissolved. Then add ice, stir again, and garnish with a lime wedge. Serve with a stirrer.

Frozen Mango & Mint Daiquiri

2 measures white rum
½ measure mango liqueur
1 measure freshly squeezed lime juice

1 dash sugar syrup
½ ripe mango
1 mint sprig, to garnish

Blend all of the ingredients with a small scoop of crushed ice and pour into a hurricane glass. Garnish with a sprig of mint.

Banana Daiquiri

2 measures white rum
½ measure banana liqueur
1 measure freshly squeezed lime juice

1 dash sugar syrup
½ ripe banana
banana slices, to garnish

Blend all of the ingredients with a small scoop of crushed ice and pour into a hurricane glass. Garnish with slices of banana.

Ripe for delight Pick the wrong banana or a too-young mango, and your Daiquiri could be ruined. Bananas should be a strong yellow with no hint of green. A melon should be soft if pressed at either end; a ripe passion fruit's skin should be crinkled, not smooth; and a mango's flesh should be bright yellow and moist if it is ripe. It will be drier and greener if it is not. Make sure your fruit is ripe to make your Daiquiri delightful!

Strawberry Daiquiri

2 measures white rum
½ measure strawberry liqueur
1 measure freshly squeezed
lime juice

1 dash strawberry syrup
4 ripe strawberries
1 split strawberry, to garnish

Blend all of the ingredients with
a small scoop of crushed ice and
pour into a hurricane glass.
Garnish with a split strawberry
on the rim of the glass.

Flexible friends Daiquiris and Bellinis are two of the most adaptable
cocktails. Stick to the basic principles and you can experiment with a
variety of your favorite fruits and flavors to make your own original and
delicious drinks.

Melon Daiquiri

2 measures white rum
½ measure Midori (melon liqueur)
1 measure freshly squeezed
lime juice

1 dash sugar syrup
6 chunks ripe Galia melon
2 slices Galia melon, to garnish

Blend all of the ingredients with a small scoop of crushed ice and pour
into a hurricane glass. Garnish with the melon slices.

Spiced Raspberry Daiquiri

2 measures Morgan Spiced Rum
1 measure raspberry purée
1 measure freshly squeezed
lime juice

1 dash sugar syrup
lime wedges, to garnish

Shake all of the ingredients with ice and strain into an ice-filled old-fashioned glass. Garnish with lime wedges.

A case of mistaken identity Morgan's Spiced Rum is a wonderfully aromatic cocktail ingredient. It's a little-known fact, however, that this rum isn't a rum. Under EU law it isn't recognized as such, because its alcohol content is less then 37.5%. It still tastes wonderful, though!

Daiquiri Mulata

2 measures aged rum
(such as Havana 7-year old)
1 measure freshly squeezed
lime juice

1 measure dark crème de cacao
(chocolate-flavored liqueur)
1 dash sugar syrup

Blend all of the ingredients with a small scoop of crushed ice and serve in a chilled goblet, with straws.

Hemingway Daiquiri (Papa Doble)

3 measures white rum
1 measure freshly squeezed
lime juice

1 measure freshly squeezed
grapefruit juice
1 dash maraschino liqueur
(cherry liqueur)

Blend all of the ingredients with
a small scoop of crushed ice and
serve in a large highball glass
with straws.

The explorer's cocktail
Want a cocktail that makes you
feel adventurous? The Papa
Hemingway was invented for
the famous explorer, author, and
drinker, Ernest Hemingway, at
the Floridita in Havana, Cuba—
which is also the home of the
Daiquiri. Hemingway's regular
stool still sits there, reserved
and empty.

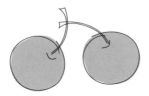

Presidente

2 measures white rum
½ measure dry vermouth
½ measure sweet vermouth

1 dash triple sec
1 orange twist

Stir all of the liquid ingredients in a mixing glass with ice until thoroughly chilled. Strain into a chilled martini glass, squeeze the orange twist over the drink, and drop in.

Keep it clean Many cocktail recipes ask you to "stir with ice and strain," but what's the best way of doing this without making a mess? Firstly, pour the ingredients into a mixing glass and then add the ice. Use a long bar spoon (ideally with a twisted handle) and gently stir the drink until thoroughly chilled. Then use a Hawthorne strainer to strain the drink into the glass, usually a chilled martini glass.

Rum Martini

½ measure dry vermouth
2 measures white rum

1 lemon twist, to garnish

This drink is strictly for the rum-lover. Fill a mixing glass with ice and add the vermouth. Stir to coat the ice and discard any liquid. Add the rum to the flavored ice and stir to chill thoroughly. Strain into a frozen martini glass and garnish with a twist of lemon.

White Witch

1 measure white rum
½ measure white crème de cacao
(chocolate-flavored liqueur)
½ measure Cointreau

1 dash freshly squeezed lime juice
soda water, to top
1 lime wedge and 1 orange wedge,
  to garnish

Shake the rum, crème de cacao, Cointreau, and lime juice together
and strain into an ice-filled old-fashioned glass. Top with soda and stir.
Garnish with lime and orange wedges, and serve with straws.

Scorpion

1 measure dark rum
½ measure white rum
½ measure Cointreau
½ measure freshly squeezed
  lime juice

2 measures freshly squeezed
  orange juice
1 dash sugar syrup
orange slices, to garnish

Shake all of the liquid ingredients with ice and strain into an ice-filled
highball glass. Garnish with orange slices and serve with straws.

Mai Tai

2 measures aged rum (such as
Appleton VX)
1 measure orange curaçao
½ measure freshly squeezed
lime juice

½ measure orgeat syrup
(almond syrup)
1 mint sprig, to garnish

Shake all of the ingredients
briefly with ice and strain
over crushed ice in a large
old-fashioned glass. Garnish
with a sprig of mint and serve
with straws.

Sister cocktails The original Mai Tai recipe dates back to the end
of World War II when *Trader Vic's* was opened. The Zombie was also
invented around the same time, and the two recipes are often confused.

Batiste

2 measures gold rum
1 measure Grand Marnier

1 orange twist, to garnish

Stir the liquids with ice until thoroughly chilled and strain into a
chilled martini glass. Garnish with a twist of orange.

Zombie

1 measure gold rum
1 measure white rum
½ measure apricot brandy
2 dashes freshly squeezed lime juice
2 measures pineapple juice

1 measure freshly squeezed orange juice
1 dash sugar syrup
1 dash Woods Navy Rum (over-proof dark rum)
1 pineapple leaf and 1 orange slice, to garnish

Shake all of the ingredients, except the dark rum, briefly with ice and strain into a large ice-filled hurricane glass. Float the dark rum on the surface of the cocktail, garnish with a pineapple leaf and an orange slice, then serve with long straws.

Zombie Prince

1 measure gold rum
1 measure white rum
1 measure freshly squeezed orange juice
1 measure freshly squeezed grapefruit juice

½ measure freshly squeezed lemon juice
4 drops of Angostura bitters
2 pink grapefruit slices, to garnish

Build all of the ingredients over crushed ice in a highball glass. Transfer the contents to a shaker, briefly shake, and return to the glass, unstrained. Garnish with the slices of pink grapefruit.

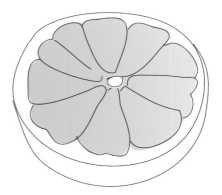

Honeysuckle

1 measure Creole Shrub Rum
1 measure gold rum
$\frac{1}{2}$ measure freshly squeezed
lime juice

$\frac{1}{2}$ measure liquid orange
blossom honey
4 drops orange bitters
1 flamed orange twist, to garnish

Shake all of the ingredients with ice and strain into a chilled martini glass. Garnish with a flamed orange twist.

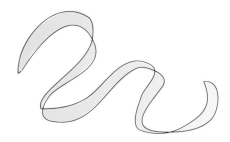

Cuba Libre

2 measures white rum
$\frac{1}{2}$ lime

Coca-Cola, to top

Add the rum to an ice-filled highball glass. Cut the lime into four segments and squeeze into the drink, dropping each one in. Top with Coca-Cola, stir, and serve with straws.

Building blocks You don't need a hard hat to "build" a cocktail. This simply means pouring your different ingredients directly into the serving glass. Usually over ice and stirred before serving.

Rum Alexander

1 measure dark rum
1 measure dark crème de cacao
(chocolate-flavored liqueur)

1 measure heavy cream
ground nutmeg

Shake all of the liquid ingredients with ice and strain into a chilled martini glass. Sprinkle the nutmeg on the surface of the drink.

Tre

2 measures gold rum
1 measure freshly pressed
apple juice
2 dashes Chambord (black
raspberry liqueur)

1 dash sugar syrup
1 lime twist, to garnish

Add all of the ingredients to a mixing glass, then fill with ice. Stir to chill thoroughly, then strain into a frozen martini glass. Adjust the sweetness by taste. Garnish with a lime twist.

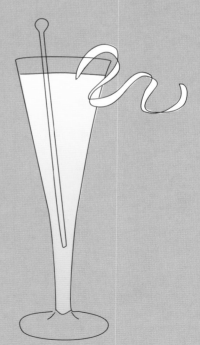

Mojito

8 mint leaves	2 measures white rum
½ lime	1 dash soda water
2 dashes sugar syrup	1 sprig of mint, to garnish

In the base of a highball glass, muddle the mint, lime, and sugar syrup. Fill the glass with crushed ice and add the rum. Stir, then add a dash of soda water. Garnish with a mint sprig and serve with long straws.

In a muddle "Muddling" is the term used for the process by which a fruit or herb is crushed to release its flavors. The cocktail maker uses a blunt ended tool, similar to a pestle. And its name? A muddler.

Black Widow

1½ measures dark rum	2 dashes sugar syrup
1 measure Southern Comfort	4 drops Angostura bitters
½ measure freshly squeezed lime juice	1 lime wedge, to garnish

Shake all of the ingredients with ice and strain into a chilled martini glass. Garnish with a wedge of lime on the rim of the glass.

Apple-soaked Mojito

8 mint leaves	2 measures gold rum
½ lime	freshly pressed apple juice, to top
2 dashes sugar syrup	1 sprig of mint, to garnish

In the base of a mixing glass, muddle the mint, lime, and sugar syrup. Add the rum to this mixture and shake without ice. Fill a highball glass with crushed ice and strain the mixture over it. Then, top with the apple juice, stir, and garnish with the sprig of mint. Serve with long straws.

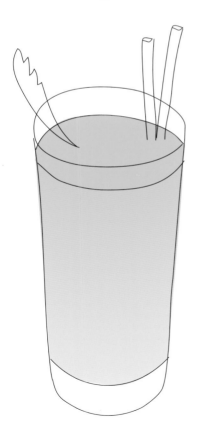

Take the strain Some drinkers prefer their Mojitos free of floating mint, in which case using a strainer is the best way to prepare the cocktail. This method of shaking the sugar, lime, mint, and rum together also really intensifies the flavors. But they should be shaken without ice, so as not to over-dilute.

Pale Treasure

1 measure white rum | bitter lemon, to top
1 measure cherry brandy | lemon slices, to garnish

Fill an old-fashioned glass with ice, add the rum and cherry brandy, and top with the bitter lemon. Stir and garnish with lemon slices.

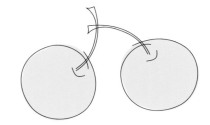

Fidel's Mojito

8 mint leaves | 2 measures white rum
½ lime, segmented | beer, to top
2 dashes sugar syrup | 1 sprig of mint, to garnish

In the base of a highball, muddle the mint, lime, and sugar syrup. Fill the glass with crushed ice and add the rum. Stir, then top with beer. Garnish with a mint sprig and serve with long straws.

Castro's cocktail twist As rumour has it, this is the way "The Beard" demands that his Mojitos are made—exactly the same as the classic but topped with beer. (After all, he is a man of the people.) Use a Cuban beer for authenticity, such as Hatuey (pronounced ah-tway).

Cuban SideCar

1 measure white rum
1 measure freshly squeezed lime juice

1 measure triple sec
1 lime twist, to garnish

Shake all of the ingredients with ice and strain into a chilled martini glass. Garnish with a lime twist.

Florida Sky

1 measure gold rum
4 mint leaves
1 dash freshly squeezed lime juice

1 measure pineapple juice
soda water, to top
slices of cucumber, to garnish

Shake the rum, mint, lime, and pineapple together with ice and strain into a highball glass over ice. Top with soda water and stir. Garnish with slices of cucumber.

The heated ice debate When adding ice, many bartenders will tell you to put your ice in the shaker and then add your ingredients before shaking or stirring. Ignore them! All the time your ice is in the shaker it is melting. Generally ice is used to chill a drink *not* to dilute it, so the less time the ice is in contact with your concoction, the better. Add your ice last, just before shaking or stirring.

Ron Collins

2 measures white rum
½ measure sugar syrup (to taste)
1 measure freshly squeezed
lime juice

soda water, to top
lime wedges and cocktail
cherries, to garnish

Fill a highball glass with crushed ice, and then add ingredients in order—rum, sugar, lime. Stir, top with soda, and garnish with lime wedges and cocktail cherries on a swizzle stick.

Rum Times

3 drops of Angostura bitters
2 measures white rum
2 measures cranberry juice

1 dash soda water
2 lime wedges, to garnish

Drop the bitters into an old-fashioned glass, and swirl to coat the inside. Fill the glass with ice and then pour the rum and cranberry over. Top with soda and garnish with two squeezed lime wedges.

Naçional

1½ measures gold rum
1 measure apricot brandy
1 measure pineapple juice

1 dash freshly squeezed lime juice
fresh apricot slices, to garnish

Shake all of the ingredients
together with ice and strain into
a chilled martini glass. Garnish
with slices of fresh apricot.

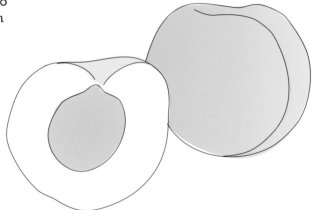

T&T Fizz

2 measures gold rum
1 measure light cream
1 measure freshly squeezed
orange juice

1 dash freshly squeezed
 lemon juice
1 dash sugar syrup
1 dash soda water
orange slices, to garnish

Shake the first five ingredients with ice and strain into a goblet.
Add a dash of soda water and garnish with the orange slices.
Serve with straws.

Cuballini

1 measure white rum
1 dash peach brandy
1 dash freshly squeezed orange juice

1 dash freshly squeezed lime juice
1 dash sugar syrup
Champagne, to top
fresh peach wedges, to garnish

Shake all but the Champagne briefly with ice and strain into a large Champagne saucer. Top with Champagne, and garnish with slices of fresh peach.

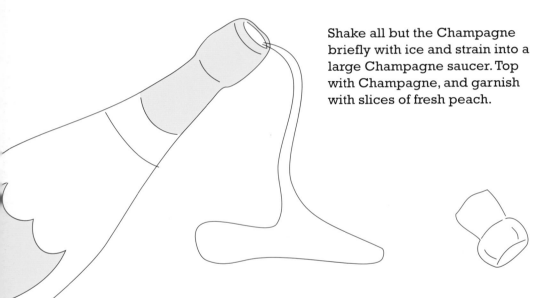

Discovery Bay

2 measures gold rum
½ measure orange curaçao
½ measure lime juice

4 drops Angostura bitters
lime wedges, to garnish

Shake all of the ingredients with ice and strain into an ice-filled highball glass. Garnish with lime wedges.

Grenada

2 measures gold rum
1 measure freshly squeezed orange juice

½ measure sweet vermouth
ground cinnamon

Shake all of the liquid ingredients with ice and strain into a chilled martini glass. Sprinkle the ground cinnamon through a flame and on to the surface of the drink.

Dandy

1 measure white rum
½ measure peach brandy
1 dash freshly squeezed orange juice

1 dash freshly squeezed lime juice
Champagne, to top
1 lime twist, to garnish

Shake all of the ingredients except Champagne briefly with ice. Strain into a large Champagne saucer and top up with Champagne. Garnish with a lime twist.

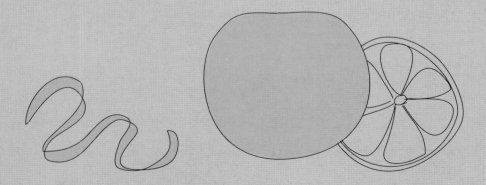

tequila

Tequila is made from the heart of the blue agave plant, a member of the lily family—not a cactus as commonly thought—and has become Mexico's National treasure. At present, there are over 500 types of tequila available to the consumer, several of which feature in this section. A common misconception is that high quality tequilas and mescals have a worm in the bottle. This is not the case however, as high quality tequila would never have such an addition—it was just an American marketing ploy introduced in the 40s!

Margarita

fine sea salt
1½ measures gold tequila
(such as Jose Cuervo Especial)

1 measure freshly squeezed
lime juice
1 measure Cointreau
1 lime wedge, to garnish

Salt the rim of a coupette (see below). Shake all of the liquid
ingredients and strain into the glass. Garnish with a lime wedge on
the rim of the glass.

Salt sensation To salt the rim of
a glass for your Margarita, firstly
moisten the outer rim with a
lime wedge, then dip and rotate
the inverted glass in fine sea
salt. Wipe the inner rim to
ensure there is no salt on this
surface as it will taint the drink.

Passion Fruit Margarita

1½ measures gold tequila
1 measure freshly squeezed
lime juice
½ measure passion fruit syrup

1 measure Cointreau
1 passion fruit, flesh only
1 lime wedge, to garnish

Shake all ingredients with
ice and strain into a coupette.
Garnish with a lime wedge
on the rim.

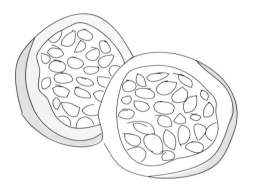

Pineapple & Mint Margarita

1½ measures gold tequila
1 measure freshly squeezed
lime juice
1 measure Cointreau

6 mint leaves
1 measure freshly pressed
pineapple juice
pineapple wedges, to garnish

Blend all of the ingredients on
high-speed in a blender, without
ice. Transfer the contents to a
shaker and shake with ice. Strain
into a large chilled martini glass
and garnish with pineapple
wedges on the rim.

Grand Margarita

pinch of fine sea salt
1½ measures gold tequila
1 measure freshly squeezed lime juice

½ measure freshly squeezed lemon juice
1 measure Grand Marnier
1 lime slice and 1 lemon slice, to garnish

Salt the rim of a large coupette (see page 100). Shake the ingredients with ice and strain into the glass. Garnish with citrus slices.

Cajun Margarita

1 measure chili-infused gold tequila
1 measure Cointreau

1 measure freshly squeezed lime juice
2 drops Tabasco sauce
1 curled red chili (see below)

Shake all ingredients with ice and strain into a large coupette. Garnish with a curled red chili.

Hot chili curls How many people do you know who can curl a chili? Follow these simple instructions if you want to impress your friends: slice the end of a chili with a sharp knife five or six times. Then leave in water for two hours. The strands will curl outward, making a great garnish.

Frozen Margarita

1 measure gold tequila
1 measure freshly squeezed
lime juice

1 measure Cointreau
1 lime slice, to garnish

Blend all of the ingredients with a
small scoop of crushed ice. Serve
in a large coupette garnished
with a lime slice.

Keeping it cool The Frozen Margarita, like the Frozen Daiquiri, should
have a fairly solid, almost sorbet-like consistency. The amount of ice used
in the blending determines the consistency, so practice makes perfect.

Frozen Strawberry Margarita

4 ripe strawberries
1 measure gold tequila
1 measure freshly squeezed
lime juice

½ measure Cointreau
½ measure strawberry liqueur
1 split strawberry

Blend all of the ingredients
with a small scoop of
crushed ice. Serve in a large
coupette garnished with a
split strawberry on the rim.

Tequila Sunrise

2 measures silver tequila
4 measures freshly squeezed
orange juice

1 dash grenadine
orange slices, to garnish

Fill a highball glass with ice, add the tequila and orange juice, then slowly drop in the grenadine which will settle at the bottom of the drink. Garnish with orange slices and serve with straws.

Frozen Tequila Sunset

1½ measures gold tequila
3 measures frozen orange juice
concentrate

1 dash passion fruit syrup
1 dash grenadine
orange slices, to garnish

Blend all of the ingredients, except the grenadine, with a small scoop of crushed ice. Pour the blended mixture into a highball glass, garnish with orange slices and before serving, drizzle the grenadine over the surface.

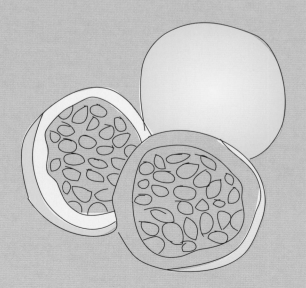

Pale Original

2 measures gold tequila
1 measure guava juice
1 measure freshly squeezed
lime juice

2 dashes ginger syrup
1 lime wedge, to garnish

Shake all of the ingredients with ice and strain into a chilled martini glass. Garnish with the lime wedge on the rim of the glass.

Cancun Crush

2 lime wedges
2 lemon wedges
½ measure passion fruit syrup
2 measures gold tequila

½ measure Passoã (passion fruit
    liqueur)
1½ measures peach juice

In the base of a shaker, muddle one lemon wedge and one lime wedge with the passion fruit syrup. Add the tequila, Passoã, peach juice, and a scoop of crushed ice. Shake briefly and transfer, unstrained, into a highball glass. Garnish with the remaining fruit wedges.

Danish passion Passoã is a passion-fruit flavored liqueur with a tropical taste. And who invented it? The Danes. The luscious texture is balanced by an acidic grapefruit note, which works wonderfully with tequila.

Easy Tiger

2 measures gold tequila
1 measure freshly squeezed
lime juice

2 teaspoons liquid honey
2 teaspoons ginger cordial
1 orange twist, to garnish

Add all of the ingredients to a mixing glass and stir until the honey has dissolved. Then add ice, shake, and strain into a chilled Champagne flute. Garnish with an orange twist.

Sweet as honey All bartenders have a pot of honey hidden away somewhere around their bar. It dissolves in a cocktail much easier than sugar would. But even so, make sure you warm it before stirring it with other ingredients—it will dissolve even more quickly. And time is of the essence when your guests have worked up a thirst!

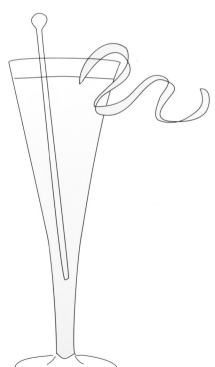

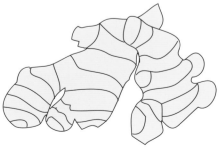

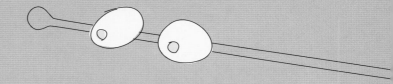

Tequini

3 measures silver tequila | ½ measure dry vermouth
3 drops orange bitters | 2 black olives, to garnish

Pour all of the ingredients into a mixing glass, add ice, and stir until thoroughly chilled. Strain into a frozen martini glass and garnish with two black olives on a swizzle stick.

Vampiro

2 measures gold tequila | 1 dash sugar syrup
1 measure tomato juice | 1 dash Worcestershire sauce
2 dashes lime juice | celery salt

Pour all of the ingredients into a mixing glass, add ice, and stir until thoroughly chilled. Rim a martini glass with celery salt and strain the cocktail into it.

Desperado

½ lime, cut into segments | dark beer, to top
1 tablespoon brown sugar | 1 measure gold tequila

Muddle the lime and sugar in the base of a large highball glass. Fill with ice and slowly pour the beer and tequila over. Stir, and serve.

Tijuana Sling

1½ measures gold tequila
½ measure crème de cassis
(black currant liqueur)
½ measure freshly squeezed
lime juice

2 drops Peychaud's bitters
(herbal liqueur)
ginger ale, to top
1 lime slice and blueberries,
to garnish

Pour the tequila, cassis, lime juice, and bitters into a shaker and shake with ice. Strain this into an ice-filled sling glass, top with ginger ale and garnish with the lime slice and blueberries. Serve with straws.

Cocktail therapy You could use an automatic ice crusher to get your crushed ice. But that would be boring. It's far more fun to put your ice in a heavy plastic bag and take a rolling pin to it! Pound away until the ice is the right consistency. You'll have a nice, cool drink *and* you'll have worked out a lot of your pent-up aggression!

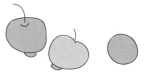

Thigh High

1 measure gold tequila
1 measure dark crème de cacao
(chocolate-flavored liqueur)
1 measure light cream

3 strawberries
1 dash strawberry syrup
cocoa powder and 1 split
strawberry, to garnish

Blend all of the ingredients with a small scoop of crushed ice and serve in a hurricane glass. Dust the strawberry with a little cocoa powder and place it on the rim of the glass as a garnish.

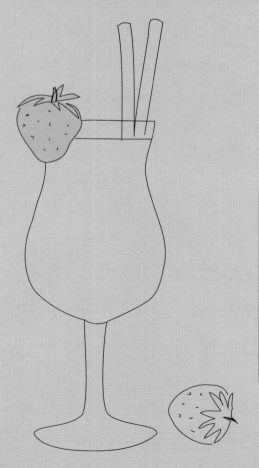

Too late to taste If your cocktail is in the glass and garnished, it's too late to make sure you've got your quantities right. You don't want to hand the finished article over and watch a drinker's face pucker up! Always taste a cocktail before pouring it out. This means you can adjust the sweet/sour balance by adding either more sugar syrup or lime juice—and you've averted a taste disaster.

Border Crossing

1½ measures gold tequila
1 measure freshly squeezed
lime juice
1 measure liquid honey

4 drops orange bitters
bitter lemon, to top
lemon slices, to garnish

Shake the first four ingredients with ice and strain into a sling glass. Top with bitter lemon, stir, and garnish with lemon slices. Serve with long straws.

Off-Shore

1 measure gold tequila
1 measure white rum
6 mint leaves
3 chunks fresh pineapple

2 measures pineapple juice
1 measure light cream
1 mint sprig, to garnish

Blend all of the ingredients with a small scoop of crushed ice and serve in a hurricane glass. Garnish with a mint sprig and serve with straws.

Forest Fruit

1 lime wedge	2 teaspoons crème de mure
fine brown sugar	(blackberry liqueur)
2 blackberries	1½ measures silver tequila
2 raspberries	½ measure Cointreau
2 teaspoons Chambord (black	1 measure freshly squeezed
raspberry liqueur)	lemon juice
	lemon slices, to garnish

Moisten the rim of a large old-fashioned glass with the lime wedge and coat with brown sugar. In the glass, muddle the fresh berries with the Chambord and crème de mure. Fill the glass with crushed ice. Now, add the tequila, Cointreau, and lemon juice. Stir to mix thoroughly, garnish with lemon slices, and serve with straws.

Sour Apple

1½ measures gold tequila	1 measure freshly pressed
2 dashes Cointreau	apple juice
½ measure apple schnapps	1 apple wedge, to garnish
½ measure freshly squeezed	
lime juice	

Shake all ingredients with ice and strain into a chilled martini glass. Garnish with the slice of apple on the rim.

Baja Sour

1½ measures gold tequila	½ egg white (see page 69)
2 drops orange bitters	1 dash dry sherry
1 measure lemon juice	lemon slices, to garnish
½ measure sugar syrup	

Shake all of the ingredients, except the sherry, with ice and strain into an ice-filled old-fashioned glass. Drizzle over the sherry and garnish with slices of lemon.

Holdscock

2 dashes chilled Goldschlager (cinnamon liqueur)	1 orange wedge
	ground cinnamon
1 measure chilled gold tequila	

Layer the tequila on top of the Goldschlager, place an orange wedge across the rim of the glass, and sprinkle ground cinnamon, through a flame, over it. Drink the shot and then bite the garnish.

Dripping gold Goldschlager is a cinnamon liqueur, which has the added novelty of edible gold leaf flakes that swirl round in the bottle.

Tequila Slammer

1 dash dark crème de cacao	1 measure Champagne
(chocolate-flavored liqueur)	1 measure gold tequila

Pour all of the ingredients into a heavy-based old-fashioned glass. Instruct the drinker to cover the glass with their hand, bang the glass on a hard surface, and down the contents in one.

Slam sensation The wonderful intoxicating power of "slammers" comes from the fact that the alcohol dissolves in the bubbles created by the shock of slamming the glass down, and so is absorbed into the blood stream much more quickly. Slammers can be made using any kind of fizzy mixer, such as Champagne, soda, lemonade, cider, or bitter lemon.

Kalashnikov

1 orange slice	ground coffee
fine white sugar	1 measure gold tequila

Dip the orange slice in fine white sugar and then sprinkle ground coffee over it. Instruct the drinker to suck the flavored orange, drink the shot, then bite the orange.

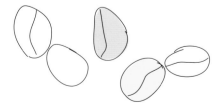

Many different types of whiskey exist, including Scotch, Irish, Rye, Canadian, Japanese, and Bourbon. It is a barrel-aged, distilled spirit, produced from grain or malt. Scotch can only be so-named if it is made in Scotland. Bourbon is named after Bourbon County, Kentucky, where it originated. The name whiskey derives originally from the Gaelic "uisge beatha," meaning, "water of life." Although many prefer to drink whiskey on its own, why not try it as a cocktail ingredient? It needs careful planning and execution but can work wonders if done well.

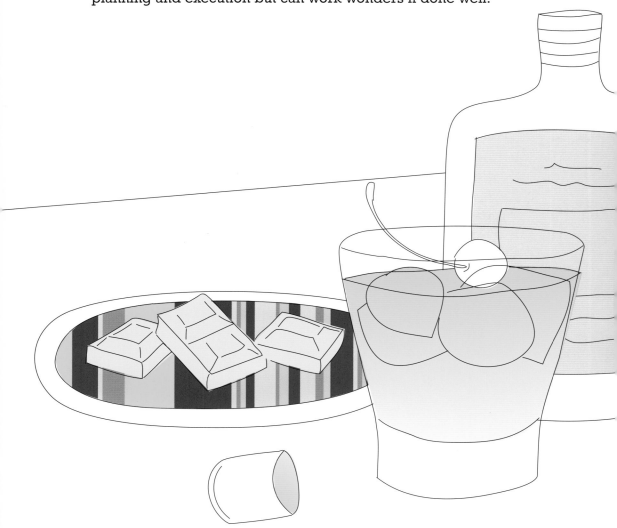

whiskey

Sweet Whisky Fuel

1 measure chilled Scotch whisky
4 drops Angostura bitters
2 measures Champagne

2 measures chilled Red Bull
(energy drink)
1 orange twist, to garnish

Pour the whisky and bitters into a Champagne flute, add the Champagne, and then Red Bull. Garnish with an orange twist and stir before serving.

Zoom

2 measures Scotch whisky
1 large teaspoon liquid honey

1 measure chilled water
1 measure heavy cream

Shake all of the ingredients with ice and strain into a chilled martini glass.

Shake, rattle 'n' roll If you want to shake things up a bit, how do you know when you've done enough shaking? Pour your cocktail ingredients into a shaker, add the ice. and shake until a frost forms on the outer surface of the shaker. When things turn frosty, your cocktail is just cool enough. Strain the drink into the serving glass, double straining through a tea strainer if specified.

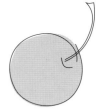

Whiskey Sour

2 measures Bourbon	½ egg white (optional, see page 69)
1 measure freshly squeezed lemon juice	1 cocktail cherry and 1 lemon slice, to garnish
1 measure sugar syrup	

Shake all of the ingredients with ice and strain into an ice-filled old-fashioned glass. Garnish with a lemon slice and a cherry.

Pure and simple A Whiskey Sour is one of the simplest and most classic drinks available. It can be made with any whiskey, but it is my personal opinion that this drink is at its finest using good, old-fashioned Bourbon. A great drink!

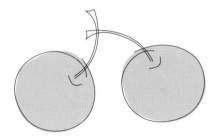

Whisky Mac

2 measures Scotch whisky | 1½ measures ginger wine

Pour both ingredients over ice in an old-fashioned glass and stir to mix.

Sazerac

1 measure absinthe	½ measure sugar syrup
chilled water, to top	6 drops Peychaud's bitters
1 measure Bourbon	(herbal liqueur)
1 measure cognac	4 drops Angostura bitters

Pour the absinthe into an old-fashioned glass over ice, and fill with water. Meanwhile shake the Bourbon, cognac, and bitters with ice. Discard the liquid in the old-fashioned glass, and strain the cocktail into it (straight up).

Down the drain In the good old days, a good cocktail came at any expense. Bartenders would happily throw absinthe down the sink. How come? Well, traditionally the first step in making a Sazerac is to swill absinthe around in the glass—and then pour it out. This gives just the right hint of absinthe—no more, no less.

Old-Fashioned

2 measures Bourbon
4 drops Angostura bitters

2 teaspoons sugar syrup
1 orange twist, to garnish

The key to this wonderful cocktail is dilution by stirring. Add the sugar syrup and bitters to an old-fashioned glass, and stir with two ice cubes. Then add the Bourbon, bit by bit, along with more ice, stirring constantly. Garnish with an orange twist and serve with a stirrer.

To "e" or not to "e" You think whisky (or whiskey) is straightforward? Generally, whisky made in Scotland (i.e. Scotch whisky) has no "e" in its spelling. If made outside Scotland it is spelt "whiskey." The two exceptions are Canadian and Japanese whisky. This is because a Scotsman first introduced whisky to Canada in 1799, and Masataka Taketsuru learnt his trade in Glasgow distilleries before returning to Japan.

Cinnamon Old-Fashioned

1½ measures Bourbon
1 measure Goldschlager
(cinnamon-flavored liqueur)

1 teaspoon brown sugar
5 drops orange bitters
1 cinnamon stick, to garnish

Pour over ice in an old-fashioned glass, stir, and serve with a cinnamon stick as garnish.

Manhattan

**2 measures Bourbon or
rye whiskey
½ measure sweet vermouth**

**4 drops Angostura bitters
1 cocktail cherry, to garnish**

Stir the whiskey, vermouth, and bitters with ice until thoroughly chilled. Then strain into a chilled martini glass and garnish with a cocktail cherry on a swizzle stick.

Harlequin

**7 white seedless grapes
6 drops orange bitters**

**2 measures Canadian whisky
½ measure sweet vermouth**

Muddle five of the grapes with the bitters in an old-fashioned glass. Fill with crushed ice and add the whisky. Stir, re-top with crushed ice, and lace with vermouth. Garnish with the two remaining grapes and serve with straws.

Silky Pin

1 measure Scotch whisky
1 measure Drambuie Cream

Pour the ingredients over ice in
an old-fashioned glass and serve
with a stirrer.

Mint Julep

6 mint leaves | 4 drops Angostura bitters
2 dashes sugar syrup | 2 measures Bourbon

In the base of a highball glass,
bruise the mint leaves with the
sugar syrup and bitters. Fill the
glass with crushed ice and add
the Bourbon. Stir well and serve
with straws and a cocktail napkin
wrapped around the glass.

Keeping cool When you've gone to all the trouble of mixing a long drink
over crushed ice like the Julep, or the Mojito (see page 90), you can't let
anything ruin it! So it's a good idea to serve these drinks with a cocktail
napkin wrapped around the glass—otherwise the heat from your hand
will quickly melt the ice, over-diluting the drink. And you should never
over-dilute a cocktail!

Godfather Sour

1½ measures Bourbon
1 measure amaretto
1 measure freshly squeezed
lemon juice

1 dash sugar syrup
1 egg white (see page 69)
4 drops Angostura bitters
lemon slices, to garnish

Shake all of the ingredients with ice and strain into an ice-filled old-fashioned glass. Garnish with lemon slices and serve with straws.

Algonquin

2 measures rye whiskey
1 measure dry vermouth
1½ measure pineapple juice

4 drops Peychaud's bitters
(herbal liqueur)

Shake all ingredients with ice and strain into an ice-filled old-fashioned glass.

Swallow your medicine Like Angostura bitters, Peychaud's bitters started life in the medicine cabinet. But, like a lot of ingredients now used in my bar, the medicinal qualities have long since been forgotten.

Solera Eclipse

2 measures single malt whiskey (such as Glenfiddich Solera Reserve)
1 dash sweet vermouth

1 dash dry vermouth
4 drops Angostura bitters
1 cocktail cherry and 1 mint sprig, to garnish

Shake the ingredients with ice and strain over crushed ice. Drop a cherry into the drink and garnish with a mint sprig.

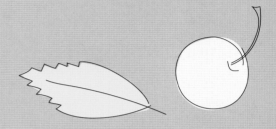

Rhett Butler

2 measures Bourbon
4 measures cranberry juice

2 lime wedges

Pour the ingredients over ice in an old-fashioned glass. Squeeze the limes and drop into the drink. Serve with a stirrer.

Raspberry Lynchburg

2 measures Jack Daniels
½ measure Chambord (black raspberry liqueur)
1 measure freshly squeezed lime juice

1 measure raspberry purée
1 dash sugar syrup
lemonade, to top
3 raspberries, to garnish

Shake the first five ingredients together and strain over ice into a highball glass. Top with lemonade and stir. Garnish with the raspberries and serve with straws.

At home with Jack Lynchburg, Tennessee is the home of Jack Daniels. This small country town is the site for the distillation of every single drop of the world's most popular whiskey, which is definitely not a bourbon. Why it is called Jack Daniel's No. 7? Nobody knows!

Lynchburg Lemonade

1½ measure Jack Daniels
1 measure triple sec
1 measure freshly squeezed
lemon juice

lemonade, to top
lemon slices, to garnish

Shake the Jack Daniels, triple sec, and lemon juice together with ice and strain over ice into a tall highball glass. Top with lemonade, stir, and garnish with lemon slices. Serve with straws.

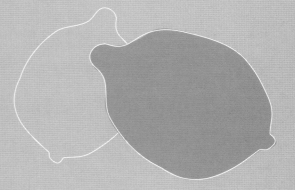

Aggravation

1½ measures Scotch whisky
1 measure Kahlua (coffee liqueur)
1 measure heavy cream

1 measure milk
ground nutmeg, for dusting

Shake all liquids briefly with ice and strain into an ice-filled old-fashioned glass. Dust the surface of the drink with ground nutmeg.

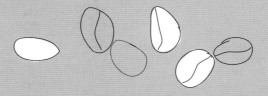

Bourbon Cookie

2 measures Bourbon
½ measure heavy cream
½ measure milk

½ measure mango syrup
½ measure butterscotch schnapps
ground cinnamon

Shake liquid ingredients with ice and double strain into an ice-filled old-fashioned glass. Dust the surface with cinnamon.

Apple Crumble Martini

1½ measures Scotch whisky
½ measure butterscotch schnapps
1 measure freshly pressed apple juice

½ measure freshly squeezed lemon juice
1 dash sugar syrup
1 apple wedge, to garnish

Shake all of the liquid ingredients with ice and double strain into a chilled martini glass. Garnish with a wedge of apple on the rim of the glass.

Simple Syrup The simplest homemade syrup is called exactly that. Make it in the following way:
2 parts fine white sugar
1 part boiling water
Stir to dissolve and leave refrigerated to cool. Although it only has a four-day shelf life, which is much less then commercially-produced syrups, it's a great sugar syrup.

Nutty Nashville

2 teaspoons liquid honey
1 measure Bourbon
½ measure Frangelico
½ measure krupnik vodka
(honey vodka)
1 lemon twist, to garnish

Stir the honey with the Bourbon in the base of a shaker to dissolve. Then add the remaining ingredients and shake with ice. Double strain the mix into chilled a champagne saucer and garnish with a lemon twist.

Bridalise

2 measures Bourbon
½ measure elderflower cordial
1 dash rose water
1 edible flower, to garnish

Shake all of the liquid ingredients together, strain into a chilled martini glass, and garnish with the flower.

St. Lawrence

2 measures Bourbon
1 measure vanilla and cinnamon-
    infused maple syrup
2 drops Angostura bitters

1 measure freshly squeezed
    lemon juice
1 cinnamon stick, to garnish

Shake all the liquid ingredients
with ice and strain into an
ice-filled old-fashioned glass.
Garnish with the cinnamon stick
as a stirrer.

Sweet sensation Experimentation is the key to good cocktail-making!
Try making some of your own homemade flavored syrups: make a fresh
batch of sugar syrup (see page 126) and infuse it with whatever you like!
Go on, live a little! This process is very similar to infusing a spirit,
although not for as long. Keep the infusion refrigerated and monitor it
before using. Depending on what you have used to infuse, its shelf life
will be relatively short. This is another perfect opportunity to really
experiment and create your own cocktails.

Sir Thomas

2 measures Bourbon
1 dash orange curaçao
1 dash cherry liqueur

1 dash sweet vermouth
1 orange twist, to garnish

Stir the ingredients together with ice and strain into a chilled martini
glass. Garnish with the orange twist.

Frisky Buck

2 measures **Bourbon**
½ measure **butterscotch schnapps**

1½ measures **pineapple juice**
cocktail cherry, to garnish

Shake all of the liquid ingredients with ice and strain into a chilled martini glass. Garnish with the cherry on a swizzle stick.

Kiwi in Kentucky

1 **kiwi fruit, peeled**
2 measures **Bourbon**
1 measure **freshly squeezed lemon juice**

½ measure **kiwi liqueur**
lemonade, to top
kiwi slices, to garnish

Muddle the kiwi fruit in the base of a shaker, add the Bourbon and lemon juice, and shake with ice. Fill a highball glass with crushed ice and strain the mixture over it. Lace with the liqueur, stir, and top with lemonade. Garnish with kiwi slices and serve with straws.

The real Mccoy Bourbon can be made anywhere in the USA, but if you want to sip the real thing, then you need to go to Kentucky. Or at least to a bar that stocks Kentucky bourbon! Only the bourbon made in this US state can advertise Kentucky as its origin.

Old Thymer

2 teaspoons vanilla sugar	2 measures Bourbon
1 drop Angostura bitters	flamed orange twist (see page 18)
2 teaspoons ginger and lemon grass syrup	1 sprig of thyme, to garnish

Use gradual dilution to build this cocktail. In an old-fashioned glass, spoon the sugar, bitters, and 1 teaspoon of syrup. Stir to dissolve the sugar. Add some ice and 1 measure of Bourbon, and mix. Add more ice and the remaining Bourbon and syrup. Garnish with a flamed orange twist and the sprig of thyme. Serve with a stirrer.

Highland Sling

1½ measures Scotch whisky	2 measures freshly pressed apple juice
½ measure Galliano	1 apple wedge, to garnish
1 measure cranberry juice	
½ measure apricot brandy	

Shake all of the ingredients with ice and strain into a sling glass over ice. Garnish with an apple wedge and serve with straws.

Getting fruity Always try to use fresh fruit juices in your cocktails. This is crucial with citrus juices. Concentrates just won't cut it. Though they're harder to come by, fresh fruit juices are well worth it.

GE Blonde

1½ measures Scotch whisky
1 measure unoaked chardonnay
1 measure freshly pressed
apple juice

1 dash sugar syrup
1 dash freshly squeezed
lemon juice
1 apple wedge, to garnish

Shake all of the ingredients together with ice and strain into a chilled martini glass. Garnish with an apple wedge

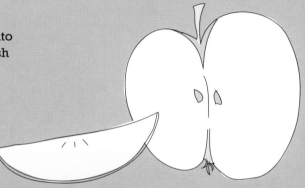

4th July

1 measure Bourbon
½ measure Galliano
ground cinnamon
½ measure Kahlua (coffee liqueur)

1 measure freshly squeezed
orange juice
½ measure heavy cream
1 cocktail cherry, to garnish

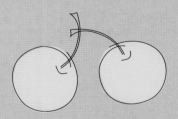

In the base of a metal shaker, ignite the Bourbon and Galliano. Now sprinkle the cinnamon over this flame. Extinguish by adding remaining ingredients and shake with ice. Strain into a martini glass and garnish with a cherry on the rim.

Mystique

1½ measures Scotch whisky
1 measure Tuaca (Italian liqueur)

1 measure Chambord (black raspberry liqueur)
1 raspberry, to garnish

Stir all of the ingredients with ice and strain into a chilled martini glass. Garnish with the raspberry.

Heaven and Hell If you have a bit of an angel *and* a bit of a devil in you, then you need to sip a Tuaca. This is an Italian brandy-based liqueur (pronounced Too-Wa-Ca). Famous for its slogan promising "sent from heaven, consumed like hell," this great ingredient has intense coffee and vanilla notes, and works wonderfully with Scotch in cocktails.

Frisco Sour

1½ measures Irish whiskey
½ measure Benedictine
1 measure freshly squeezed lemon juice

½ measure sugar syrup
1 egg white (see page 69)
2 dashes Angostura bitters
1 orange wedge

Shake all of the liquid ingredients with ice and strain into an ice-filled old-fashioned glass. Squeeze the orange wedge over the drink and then drop in as a garnish.

Morello Bourbon Daiquiri

2 measures Bourbon
1 measure Morello cherry purée
1 measure freshly squeezed
lime juice

½ measure sugar syrup
lime wedges, to garnish

Shake the first four ingredients together with ice. This drink may be
served either straight up in a martini glass or on the rocks in an
old-fashioned glass. Garnish with lime wedges.

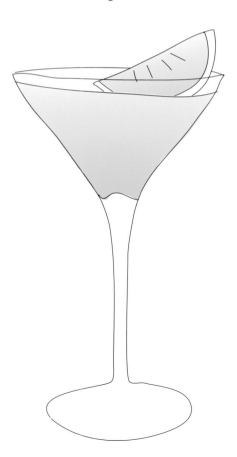

Accessorize this! You haven't
finished making a cocktail, until
you've added an accessory!
Some of the must-have garnishes
combine color, taste, and image.
Here are a few suggestions:
● try berry combo's by making
mini kebabs on cocktail sticks
● use food coloring to color
sugar or salt for coating the
cocktail glass rim
● cut fruit into wedges, slices, or
thin strips to sit on the rim of the
cocktail glass.

Chin Chin

1 measure Scotch whisky
½ measure liquid honey

½ measure freshly pressed
  apple juice
Champagne, to top

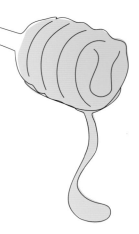

Shake first three ingredients with
ice and strain into a chilled flute.
Top with Champagne and stir
before serving.

Frontier

2 measures Bourbon
½ measure Benedictine
2 teaspoons Vanilla Madagascar
(vanilla liqueur)

2 drops Angostura bitters
1 orange twist, to garnish

As with the Old-Fashioned (see
page 119), use gradual dilution to
build and mix this drink. Garnish
with the orange twist.

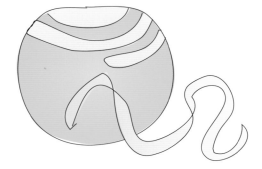

Colonel T

2 measures Bourbon | 4 measures pineapple juice
1 measure apricot brandy | 1 pineapple leaf, to garnish

Shake all of the ingredients
with ice and strain over ice
into sling glass. Garnish with
the pineapple leaf and serve
with straws.

Hoodwinked! You'd think Apricot brandy is exactly what it says it is,
wouldn't you? Think again. It isn't necessarily a brandy at all. It can be
produced by steeping apricots in brandy, but more often than not the
fruit is infused in a neutral spirit.

Toddy Royale

1 vanilla pod | 2 teaspoons maraschino
1 lemon slice | cherry juice
2 measures single malt |
Scotch whisky |

In the base of a shaker, ignite a vanilla pod briefly, then add lemon
slice and extinguish. Add the remaining ingredients and swirl to mix.
Pour unstrained over ice into an old-fashioned glass.

Kentucky Cream Tea

2 measures Bourbon
½ measure dark crème de cacao (chocolate-flavored liqueur)
1 dash krupnik vodka (honey-flavored vodka)

1 dash Cointreau
1½ measures heavy cream
2 cocktail cherries, to garnish

Fill a sling glass with crushed ice and build the ingredients in the above order. Float the cream on top and garnish with cocktail cherries on a swizzle stick.

Classic Irish Coffee

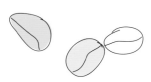

2 measures Irish whiskey
1 teaspoon sugar
hot filter coffee, to top

whipped cream
coffee beans, to garnish

Pour the coffee, sugar, and whiskey into a large wine glass. Float the cream and garnish with coffee beans.

Floating on air One of the cocktail tricks that few people know how to crack is: how do you make cream float on the surface of a drink? Well, it's not that difficult. Honestly! To float cream, whip it so that it still has a liquid quality. Then stir the drink to create a whirlpool effect and pour the cream over a spoon which is in contact with the drink's surface. Et, voila!

Derby Cream

2 measures Bourbon
1 vanilla pod
2 dashes maple syrup

1 egg white (see page 69)
½ measure heavy cream
ground cinnamon, to garnish

Shake all ingredients including the vanilla pod with ice. Strain into an ice-filled old-fashioned glass. Remove the vanilla pod and make a spiral (see below) to garnish with a sprinkle of cinnamon.

Do a twirl To make a vanilla spiral garnish, wind a vanilla pod around a straw and hold it in place for a few seconds. Release it from the straw and it should stay in a pretty spiral shape.

Loretto Lemonade

1½ measures Bourbon
½ measure Midori (melon liqueur)
½ measure freshly squeezed lime juice

1 measure freshly pressed apple juice
ginger beer, to top
1 lime wedge and 1 mint sprig, to garnish

Shake the first four ingredients with ice and strain into an ice-filled highball glass. Top with ginger beer, stir, and garnish with the mint sprig and lime wedge. Serve with straws.

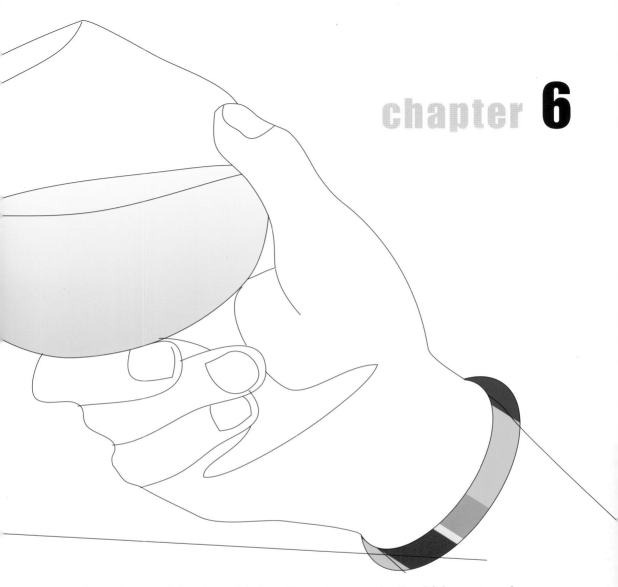

chapter 6

Brandy was introduced to Northern Europe in the 16th century by
Dutch traders. The name actually originated from the Dutch word
"brandewijn," meaning "burnt wine." Brandy is produced by
distilling grape wines, or more generally, to spirits distilled from
various fermented fruits. Fruit brandy is usually clear and colorless
and should be served chilled. Even poor quality wine can make
good brandy. Although cognac is widely recognised to be the finest
of all brandies, experiment with the different varieties used in this
chapter and delight in the versatility of brandy!

Side Car

2 measures brandy | 1 measure freshly squeezed
1 measure Cointreau | lemon juice
| 1 lemon twist

Shake all of the liquid ingredients with ice, strain over ice in a large old-fashioned glass, and garnish with a twist of lemon.

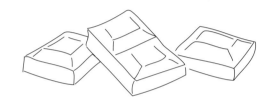

Brandy Alexander

1 measure brandy | 1 measure heavy cream
1 measure dark crème de cacao | ground nutmeg
(chocolate-flavored liqueur) |

Shake all of the ingredients with ice and strain into a chilled martini glass. Sprinkle the surface with ground nutmeg.

Short but sweet The Brandy Alexander is a heavy, sweet drink and so should be treated with respect—knock this one back too eagerly and you might start to feel a bit queasy. The original version of a Brandy Alexander was known simply as an Alexander. This cocktail used gin in place of the brandy. Today's brandy version is far more palatable.

Corpse Reviver

1½ measures brandy | ½ measure sweet vermouth
½ measure apple brandy | slices of red apple, to garnish

Shake all of the liquid ingredients with ice and strain into a chilled martini glass. Garnish the rim of the glass with slices of red apple.

An apple by any other name…
Apple brandy takes on different names depending on its origin. The French call it "calvados," most commonly produced in Normandy. Whereas in the USA, apple brandy is mostly known as "apple Jack."

brandy

Jaffa

1 measure brandy
1 measure dark crème de cacao
(chocolate-flavored liqueur)
½ measure Mandarin Napoleon

3 drops orange bitters
1 measure light cream
orange chocolate shavings,
to garnish

Shake all of the liquid ingredients with ice and strain into a chilled martini glass. Garnish the surface of the drink with orange chocolate shavings.

Nice Pear

1½ measures brandy
1 measure Poire William
(pear liqueur)

½ measure sweet vermouth
peeled pear slices, to garnish

Pour all of the liquid ingredients into a mixing glass, add ice, and stir until thoroughly chilled. Strain the mix into a frozen martini glass and garnish with slices of peeled pear.

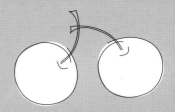

Brandy Fix

1 bar spoon confectioners' sugar	½ measure cherry brandy
1 bar spoon water	1 measure brandy
½ measure freshly squeezed lemon juice	lemon slices, to garnish

In the base of a short highball glass, stir the sugar and water together to dissolve. Then fill the glass with crushed ice and add the two brandies. Garnish with slices of lemon and serve with straws.

From the Rafters

1 measure brandy	1 measure pineapple juice
½ measure Frangelico	1 cocktail cherry, thinly sliced, to garnish
1 measure Cointreau	

Shake all of the ingredients together with ice and strain into a chilled martini glass. Float the slices of cherry in the surface foam.

A drink closer to God If you want to feel virtuous while still enjoying a cocktail, then pour yourself a shot of Frangelico. This is an Italian liqueur with a dominant hazelnut flavor and a sweet, herbal character. Its origin is reflected in its presentation: invented by a monk, the bottle is shaped like one with a length of rope tied around its waist.

Brandy Crusta

fine white sugar
2 measures brandy
½ measure orange curaçao
½ measure maraschino cherry
liqueur

1 measure freshly squeezed
lemon juice
2 drops Angostura bitters
2 cocktail cherries, to garnish

Sugar the rim of a chilled martini
glass, shake all ingredients
together with ice and strain into
the glass. Garnish with the
cherries on a swizzle stick.

Avondale Habit

3 strawberries
1 dash sugar syrup
4 mint leaves
½ teaspoon freshly cracked
black pepper

1½ measures brandy
1 dash crème de menthe
1 mint sprig and 1 split
strawberry, to garnish

Muddle the strawberries, sugar
syrup, mint leaves, and pepper in
a large old-fashioned glass. Fill
the glass with crushed ice, add the
brandy, and stir. Lace the drink
with crème de menthe and garnish
with a mint sprig and a split
strawberry. Serve with straws.

Big City Dog

1 measure brandy
½ measure Green Chartreuse
½ measure cherry brandy

3 drops Peychaud's bitters
1 orange twist, to garnish

Add the bitters to a brandy balloon glass and swirl to coat the inner surface. Pour the remaining ingredients into a mixing glass and stir with ice. Strain into the balloon and garnish with an orange twist.

The green debate If you want to see sparks fly, pull a bottle of Green Chartreuse out of your drinks cupboard. People tend to either love or loathe this French liqueur. It has a strong herbal flavor, a very high alcohol content (55%) … and a lurid green color. But it is the only green liqueur in the world with a completely natural color … and only the makers know which combination of plants produce this powerful shade of green!

Incognito

1½ measures brandy | 4 drops Angostura bitters
½ measure dry vermouth | 2 ripe apricot slices
½ measure apricot brandy |

Shake all ingredients and strain
into a chilled martini glass.
Garnish with two slices of ripe
apricot on the rim of the glass.

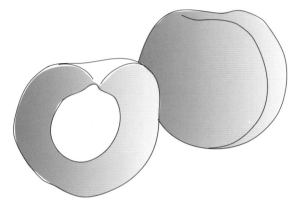

Fox Hound

2 measures brandy | ½ measure freshly squeezed
3 measures cranberry juice | lime juice
½ measure Kummel (see below) |

Shake all ingredients with ice
and strain over crushed ice into
a large goblet.

Mystery guest You may not have heard of Kummel, but it can be used to
great effect with brandy and also bourbon. It is a clear liquid distilled
from grain and flavored with caraway and anise seeds. Take it from me,
you'll want to get to know this guy!

Pisco Sour

2 measures pisco (Peruvian brandy)
1½ measures freshly squeezed lime juice
½ measure sugar syrup

½ measure fresh egg white (see page 69)
2 drops Angostura bitters
2 cocktail cherries, to garnish

Shake all of the liquid ingredients with ice and strain over crushed ice into a large old-fashioned glass. Garnish with two cherries on a swizzle stick.

Salud! Pisco is a South American brandy made from grapes, and similar in a lot of ways to grappa. It is made in Peru and Chile from high-sugar Muscat grapes.

Pisco Kid

1½ measures pisco (Peruvian brandy)
1 measure Planter's Punch Rum
1½ measures pineapple juice
4 drops orange bitters

1 dash sugar syrup
½ measure crème de mure (blackberry liqueur)
2 blackberries, to garnish

Shake the first five ingredients with ice and strain over crushed ice in an old-fashioned glass. Lace the drink with crème de mure and garnish with two blackberries. Serve with straws.

American Beauty

1 measure brandy
½ measure dry vermouth
½ measure ruby port
1 measure freshly squeezed
orange juice

1 dash sugar syrup
1 dash grenadine
1 pink rose petal, to garnish

Shake all of the liquid ingredients with ice and strain into a chilled martini glass. Garnish with a rose petal floated on the drink's surface.

Don't crack up If warming a balloon glass in which to serve a brandy, always place a metal spoon in the glass before adding boiling water. This will diffuse the heat and prevent the glass from cracking.

Apple of One's Eye

2 measures brandy
1 squeezed lime wedge
½ measure freshly pressed
apple juice

Jamaican ginger beer, to top
green apple slices, to garnish

Shake the brandy, lime, and apple juice with ice and strain into an ice-filled highball glass. Top with ginger beer, stir, and garnish with slices of green apple. Serve with straws.

Mocca

1 measure brandy
1 measure Mozart (chocolate liqueur)

1 measure Grand Marnier
1 measure milk
chocolate shavings, to garnish

Shake all of the liquid ingredients with ice and strain into a chilled martini glass. Garnish the surface with shavings of chocolate.

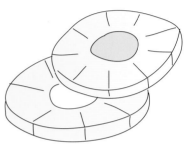

Petite Martini

2 measures VS cognac
½ measure Cointreau
1 dash sugar syrup
4 drops Angostura bitters

1 measure pineapple juice
1 caramelized pineapple slice, to garnish

Shake all of the ingredients with ice and strain into a chilled martini glass. Garnish with a slice of caramelized pineapple.

Feeling fruity What could be better than a crisp, sugary piece of fruit? Various fruits work well when caramelized, and can be used to garnish certain cocktails. To caramelize a piece of pineapple—sprinkle the surface with fine confectioners' sugar and glaze it for a brief time with a hand-held domestic blow torch until the sugar has melted and has turned slightly browned.

Sangria (traditional)

1 measure Spanish brandy	orange slices
4 measures red wine	lemon slices
4 measures lemonade	apple slices
1 measure freshly squeezed orange juice	cinnamon stick

Pour all of the ingredients into ice-filled highball glasses and garnish with pieces of the fruit. It is best made in larger quantities for a group and best consumed sitting on a beautiful sandy beach! Try and make it two hours before serving as this will give the liquid time to be infused with the fruit flavors. Just fill with fresh ice before serving.

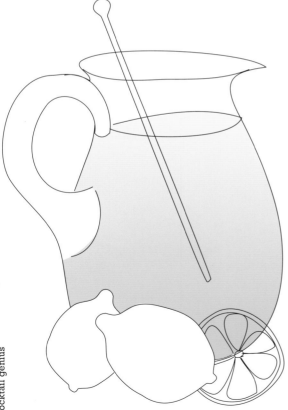

A taste of the Mediterranean
To bring a touch of the Mediterranean to your life, knock together a paella, put on a bolero and make yourself a Sangria. This classic Spanish punch varies from region to region and even from home to home. The basics are generally the same—Spanish brandy, red wine, and soda or lemonade. Beyond that any number of liqueurs, fruit juices, syrups, herbs, and spices can be used to give it your personal touch.

Dame Shamer

1½ measures brandy | 1 measure heavy cream
1 measure cherry brandy | 2 cocktail cherries, to garnish
1 measure Kahlua (coffee liqueur) |

Shake all ingredients with ice and strain into a highball glass over ice.
Garnish with two cocktail cherries on a swizzle stick.

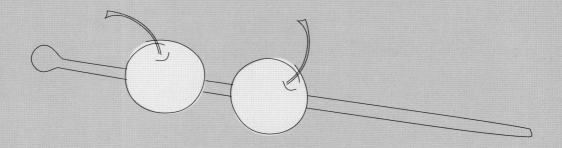

Gage's 'Secret' Sangria

1 measure Spanish brandy | 4 measures lemonade
½ measure orange curaçao | lemon wedges
½ measure gin | lime wedges
4 measures red wine | orange wedges

Fill a highball glass with ice and add the liquid ingredients. Stir
thoroughly and garnish with the pieces of fruit. This drink is better
made in larger quantities and left to infuse for a while before serving.

French 90

1 measure cognac	1 dash sugar syrup
½ measure freshly squeezed lime juice	Champagne, to top
	1 lime twist, to garnish

Shake the cognac, lime juice, and sugar syrup with ice and strain into a chilled flute. Top the mix with Champagne and garnish with a lime twist.

A step back in time Cognac is brandy—more specifically, fine brandy from the Cognac region of south-western France. Invented in the 17th century, it is double-distilled in pot stills and then aged in new oak casks. It's a real taste of France!

Red Marauder

2 measures brandy	1 dash freshly squeezed lime juice
2 measures cranberry juice	
½ measure Chambord (black raspberry liqueur)	2 raspberries, to garnish

Shake all of the ingredients with ice and strain into a chilled martini glass. Garnish with two raspberries on a swizzle stick.

Cider Apple Cooler

1½ measures apple brandy
1 measure apple schnapps

4 measures freshly pressed
apple juice
apple wedges, to garnish

Shake all ingredients with ice and strain into an ice-filled highball glass. Garnish with wedges of apple and serve with straws.

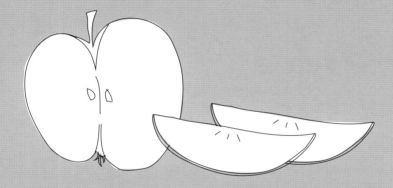

Faux Coffee Cocktail

1½ measures port
1½ measures brandy
1 egg

1 dash sugar syrup
2 drops Angostura bitters
grated nutmeg, to garnish

To make this caffeine-free cocktail shake all of the ingredients and strain into an ice-filled highball glass. Sprinkle the surface of the drink with grated nutmeg.

Cola de Mono

1-inch cinnamon stick	1 measure cold espresso
2 measures pisco	1 measure Kahlua (coffee liqueur)
(Peruvian brandy)	ground cinnamon, for dusting

Muddle the cinnamon stick with the pisco in the base of a shaker, add the other ingredients, shake with ice, and double strain into a chilled martini glass. Dust the surface with ground cinnamon.

Henry III Coffee

½ measure Kahlua (coffee liqueur)	½ measure Mandarin Napoleon
½ measure brandy	hot filter coffee, to top
½ measure Galliano	whipped cream
	ground coffee

Add the liqueurs to a toddy glass and top with hot filter coffee. Float the whipped cream on the surface and garnish with a sprinkle of ground coffee.

A hit of caffeine I can't guarantee this liqueur will keep you awake, but it will certainly put a in spring in your step! Kahlua is a Mexican coffee liqueur most commonly found in Black and White Russians (see page 14). It tastes of very sweet espresso with a hint of cocoa.

Bosom for a Pillow

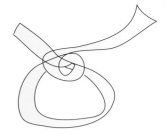

2 measures brandy	1 egg yolk
½ measure Grand Marnier	1 teaspoon grenadine
½ measure madeira	1 orange twist, to garnish

Shake all ingredients with ice and strain into a chilled martini glass. Garnish with an orange twist.

Bobbing along A busy cocktail maker might not always remember when he last filled the fridge! So to test an egg for freshness, place it in a bowl of cold water. If it is fresh, it will bob happily on the surface. If not, it will sink slowly to the bottom.

Apple Cart Martini

1½ measures apple brandy	1 dash sugar syrup
1½ measures Cointreau	apple wedge, to garnish
1 measure freshly squeezed lemon juice	

Shake all ingredients with ice and double strain into a chilled martini glass. Garnish with an apple wedge on the rim.

Brandy Blazer

| 2 measures brandy | 1 lemon twist |
| 1 orange twist | 1 white sugar cube |

Pour the brandy into a mixing glass then add the twists and sugar and flambé the mixture. Stir while ignited until the sugar has dissolved. Then double strain the mixture into a warmed brandy balloon glass.

Hands-on drinking Good brandy is often served in a balloon, also known as a "snifter." The bulbous shape of this glass means the drinking experience is enhanced by the aromas which collect above the surface of the drink. The glass is often warmed to encourage this—and the shape of the glass allows your hands to keep the drink warm as you enjoy it.

Playmate

1 measure brandy	½ egg white (see page 69)
1 measure Grand Marnier	4 drops Angostura bitters
1 measure apricot brandy	1 flaming orange twist
1 measure freshly squeezed	(see page 18)
orange juice	

Shake the liquid ingredients with ice and strain into a chilled martini glass. Flambé an orange twist over the drink and drop it in.

Champagne Classic

1 measure brandy | 6 drops Angostura bitters
1 white sugar cube | Champagne, to top

Soak the sugar cube with bitters, then add the brandy, and slowly top with Champagne. Serve with a stirrer.

Angostura bitters was originally created in the early 19th century to treat the stomach complaints of European settlers in Venezuela. It is a wonderfully aromatic ingredient with big notes of cloves, cinnamon, and medicinal herbs, blending into a rich coffee background.

Lazarus

1 measure Kahlua (coffee liqueur) | ½ measure brandy
1 measure vodka | 1 measure cold espresso

Shake all of the ingredients together with ice and strain into a chilled martini glass. There is no need to garnish this potent pick-me-up.

Pierre Collins

2 measures cognac | ½ measure sugar syrup
1 measure freshly squeezed | soda water, to top
lemon juice | lemon slices, to garnish

Shake the cognac, lemon juice, and sugar syrup with ice and strain into an ice-filled highball glass. Top with soda water, stir, and garnish with lemon slices.

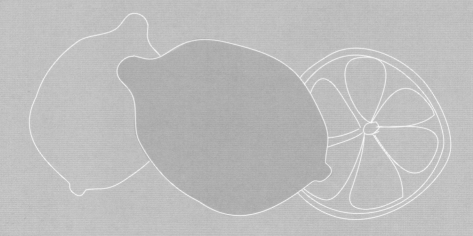

B&B

2 measures brandy
2 measures Benedictine

Build the two ingredients over ice and stir before serving. May also be served without ice in a balloon glass—a personal preference issue.

Vine

2 measures cognac
1 measure freshly pressed apple juice
½ measure freshly squeezed grapefruit juice

1 dash freshly squeezed lemon juice
1 dash sugar syrup
4 seedless grapes
grapefruit slices, to garnish

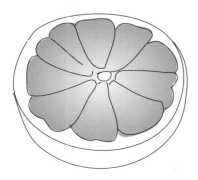

Muddle the grapes and sugar syrup in the base of a shaker. Add the remaining ingredients and shake with ice. Strain the mix over ice into a highball glass, garnish with slices of grapefruit, and serve with straws.

Peach Brandy Smash

5 or 6 mint leaves
1 teaspoon brown sugar
1 dash cold water
2 measures brandy

½ measure peach schnapps
1 mint sprig and 1 peach wedge,
to garnish

Muddle the mint, sugar, and water in the base of a shaker. Add the brandy and schnapps and shake with ice. Strain the mix over crushed ice and garnish with a wedge of ripe peach and a mint sprig. Serve with straws.

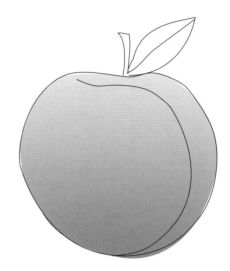

Champs Elysées

2 measures cognac
1 measure Yellow Chartreuse
½ measure freshly squeezed
lemon juice

½ measure sugar syrup
4 drops Angostura bitters
1 lemon twist, to garnish

Shake all of the ingredients with ice and strain into a chilled martini glass. Garnish with a lemon twist.

Renaissance

2 measures cognac
1 measure sweet vermouth
½ measure limoncello

5 or 6 drops peach bitters
1 lemon twist, to garnish

Shake all of the ingredients with
ice and double strain into a
chilled martini glass. Garnish
with a lemon twist.

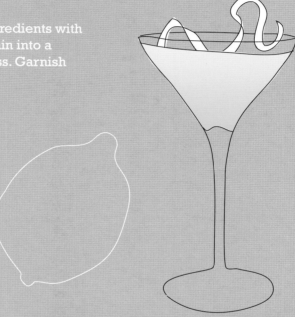

Minstrel

2 dashes cognac
2 dashes chilled vodka

1 dash crème de menthe
1 dash Kahlua (coffee liqueur)

Shake all of the ingredients very
briefly with ice and strain into a
shot glass.

The overwhelming variety of spirits available today means that it isn't necessary to stick to traditional bases, such as rum, vodka, or whiskey in order to produce a tasty cocktail. Experimenting with more exotic alcohols and finding a flavor to suit everyone's tastes couldn't be simpler. The art of cocktail-making will continue to flourish, as more and more combinations are discovered and enjoyed. Whether you are looking to celebrate, entertain, or relax, there is a creamy, refreshing, or fruity mix to suit every occasion, and selecting a favorite from this chapter won't be difficult.

best of
the rest

Natural Blonde

1 measure Bailey's Irish Cream
1 measure Grand Marnier

½ fresh mango or 1 measure
 mango purée
2 fresh mango slices, to garnish

Blend the Bailey's, Grand
Marnier, and mango together
with a small scoop of crushed
ice. Serve in a brandy balloon
glass garnished with slices of
fresh mango. Serve with short,
wide bore straws.

Batida Goiaba

2 measures cachaca (see below)
3 measures freshly squeezed (if
 possible) guava juice
1 dash sugar syrup

1 dash freshly squeezed
 lemon juice
lemon slices, to garnish

Shake all of the liquid
ingredients with ice and strain
into a highball glass filled with
crushed ice. Garnish with slices
of lemon and serve with straws.

Best of Brazil Cachaca is a Brazilian rum made from sugar cane. It is not
as pure as most rums and retains the flavor of the raw ingredient.

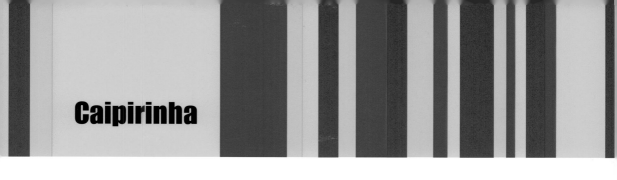

Caipirinha

1 lime, segmented
1 teaspoon brown sugar
1 dash sugar syrup

2 measures cachaca
(Brazilian rum)

In a heavy-based old-fashioned glass, muddle the lime, brown sugar, and sugar syrup. Fill the glass with crushed ice, add cachaca, stir, and serve with straws and a stirrer.

Indulge your imagination Try making a fresh fruit Caipirinha with your favorite fruit. Substitute half of the lime for four or five strawberries, or two apricots, or whatever fruit you fancy, and include a dash of the relevant fruit-based liqueur or syrup. As with every cocktail in this book—try your own twists!

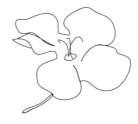

Zesty

2 measures Frangelico | 2 lime wedges

Fill a brandy balloon glass with crushed ice, add the Frangelico, then squeeze the two lime wedges into the drink, dropping them in as garnish. Serve with short straws.

Sweet Dreams The Zesty is a wonderful night-cap drink, especially in a hot climate—best enjoyed with a moonlit sea-view, if you can find one!

Toblerone

1 measure Bailey's Irish Cream | ½ measure clear liquid honey
1 measure Frangelico | 1 measure heavy cream
½ measure dark crème de cacao | 1 teaspoon chocolate sauce
(chocolate-flavored liqueur)

Blend the Bailey's, Frangelico, crème de cacao, honey, and cream with half a scoop of crushed ice. Take a hurricane glass and swirl chocolate sauce around the inner surface. Then pour in the creamy liquid and serve with straws.

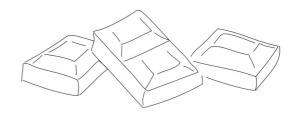

Pimms 'n' Gin Classic

1 measure Pimms No.1	lemon slices
1 measure gin	orange slices
cucumber slices	lemonade and ginger ale, to top
1 strawberry	1 mint sprig, to garnish
apple slices	

Fill a highball glass with ice, then add the Pimms and the gin. Put all of the garnishes in the glass and top with the lemonade and ginger ale. Finish off with the mint sprig and serve with straws.

Picnics with Pimms You know summer's arrived when your thoughts turn to refreshing Pimms. Scale the ingredient measurements up using the same proportions, and build over ice in the largest pitcher you can find. The flavors of the garnishes, especially the mint and cucumber, really come out here as they have longer to marinate in the drink.

Green Fairy

1 measure absinthe
1 measure freshly squeezed
lemon juice
2 drops Angostura bitters

½ egg white (see page 69)
½ measure sugar syrup
1 measure chilled water

Shake all of the ingredients with ice and strain into a chilled martini glass.

Mandarito

6 mint leaves
½ lime, cut into wedges
1 dash sugar syrup

1 measure Mandarin Napoleon
1 measure vodka
1 mint sprig, to garnish

In the base of a highball glass, muddle the mint leaves, lime wedges, and sugar syrup. Then fill the glass with crushed ice, add the liqueur and vodka, and stir. Re-fill the glass with crushed ice, garnish with a sprig of mint, and serve with straws.

The spirit of Napoleon is alive and well in the Mandarin Napoleon. This is a luscious French tangerine-based liqueur said to be invented by Napoleon 1st of France, with a bittersweet and refreshing aftertaste.

Love Junk

½ measure peach schnapps
½ measure vodka
½ measure Midori (melon liqueur)

1½ measures freshly pressed apple juice
red apple slices, to garnish

Shake all of the ingredients together with ice and strain over ice into a large old-fashioned glass. Garnish with slices of red apple.

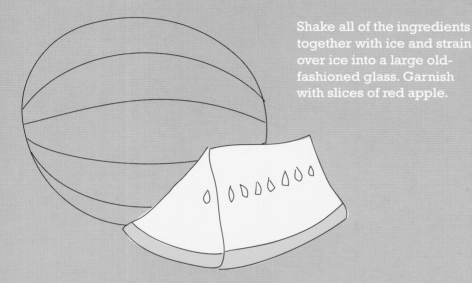

Mexican Marshmallow Mocha

2 teaspoons cocoa powder, plus a little extra as a garnish
1 measure Kahlua (coffee liqueur)

hot filter coffee, to top
2 marshmallows and whipped cream, to garnish

Put the cocoa powder in the base of a toddy glass, add the Kahlua and coffee, then stir to dissolve. Drop two marshmallows in, and float the cream over these. Dust the surface with cocoa powder.

Italian Coffee

2 measures amaretto
hot black coffee, to top

whipped cream
3 coffee beans, to garnish

Pour the amaretto and coffee into a toddy glass, then float the whipped cream on top. Garnish with three coffee beans, floating on the cream surface.

The Art of Amaretto This is an almond-based liqueur dating back to 16th-century Italy, and thought to have been created by a student of Leonardo da Vinci. The most popular brand, Disaronno, has a sweet taste of vanilla and marzipan. Leonardo would have loved it!

Coffology

1 measure cold espresso
1 measure Grand Marnier

½ measure Bailey's Irish Cream
2 orange twists, to garnish

Fill a brandy balloon glass with crushed ice and pour each ingredient over. Stir thoroughly, garnish with orange twists, and serve with a stirrer.

Class Apart

1 measure Grand Marnier
1 teaspoon brown sugar
6 drops Angostura bitters

Champagne, to top
1 orange twist, to garnish

A subtle, but beautiful twist on the original. Soak the sugar in the bitters, and place in the bottom of a Champagne flute. Add the Grand Marnier, and then top with Champagne. Garnish with an orange twist and serve with a stirrer.

Kir Royale

½ measure crème de cassis
(black currant liqueur)

Champagne, to top

Pour the cassis into a flute and top with chilled Champagne.

Sweet sensations The tasty crème de cassis is a black currant liqueur originally from France. A hugely popular drink in France is the Kir, which consists of cassis and white wine. An obvious twist from this is the Kir Royale.

Passionate Affair

½ measure **Passoã (passion fruit liqueur)**
1 dash **passion fruit syrup**

½ **passion fruit**
1 dash **freshly squeezed lime juice**
Champagne, to top

Shake all of the ingredients, except the Champagne briefly with ice, and strain into a large chilled Champagne flute. Top with Champagne and stir thoroughly prior to serving.

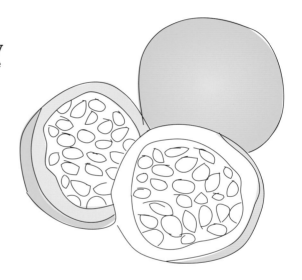

Grand Mimosa

½ measure **Grand Marnier**
1 measure **freshly squeezed orange juice**

Champagne, to top
1 **orange twist, to garnish**

Pour the Grand Marnier and orange juice into a chilled Champagne flute and stir. Top with chilled Champagne and garnish with an orange twist. Serve with a stirrer.

1 measure white peach purée | Champagne, to top
½ measure peach schnapps | 1 fresh peach wedge, to garnish

Add the peach purée and schnapps to a Champagne flute and stir to mix thoroughly. Slowly add the Champagne, stir, and garnish with a slice of fresh peach.

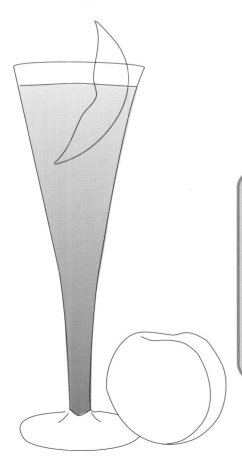

The right way to pour When pouring Champagne into a cocktail like the Bellini, use a long bar spoon with a twisted stem and a flat end. Hold the spoon vertically, spoon side up, with the flat end in contact with the purée in the flute. Then pour the Champagne down the stem of the spoon raising it as you fill the glass. Stir the cocktail before serving.

Ritz Fizz

2 dashes amaretto
2 dashes blue curaçao
2 dashes freshly squeezed
lemon juice

Champagne, to top
1 rose petal, to garnish

Pour the amaretto, curaçao, and lemon juice into a Champagne flute and top with Champagne. Stir thoroughly and float the rose petal on the drink's surface.

Tingles in your nose Champagne flutes are designed to maintain that most important ingredient of champagne—the fizz. With less surface contact, the bubbles stay intact. Ideally, chill the glass before using it.

Parisian Spring Punch

1½ measures apple brandy
½ measure Noilly Prat
(dry vermouth)
½ measure freshly squeezed
lemon juice

1 dash sugar syrup
Champagne, to top
red apple slices, to garnish

Shake all of the ingredients together briefly with ice. Strain over crushed ice in a sling glass. Top with Champagne, garnish with red apple slices, and serve with straws.

Riviera Fizz

½ measure crème de cassis
(black currant liqueur)
½ measure Poire William
(pear liqueur)

Champagne, to top
2 peeled ripe pear slices,
to garnish

Pour the cassis and Poire
William into a mixing glass,
add ice, and stir to chill. Strain
into a large martini glass and
top with Champagne. Garnish
with slices of peeled pear on
the rim of the glass.

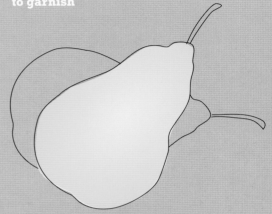

Madagascar Fizz

½ measure maraschino liqueur
½ measure Madagascar vanilla
(vanilla liqueur)

Champagne, to top
1 cocktail cherry, to garnish

Build the liqueurs in a chilled
flute, top with Champagne, and
garnish with a cocktail cherry on
a swizzle stick.

Maraschino cherries are bitter tasting fruit first distilled in Sardinia in
the early 19th century. Maraschino liqueur often shows hints of black
currant and vanilla with a big chocolate cherry finish.

Cherry Aid

½ measure absinthe
½ measure Wisniowka Cherry (cherry-flavored vodka)
½ measure sloe gin
1 dash sugar syrup

1 dash maraschino liqueur
1 dash freshly squeezed lemon juice
Champagne, to top
1 cocktail cherry, to garnish

Shake all of the ingredients except the Champagne with ice and strain into a large flute. Top with Champagne and garnish with a cocktail cherry.

The green fairy Absinthe was very popular around the end of the 19th century and sent more than a few French artistes crazy! Toulouse-Lautrec was a big fan. It is now illegal in several countries due to its high alcohol content. It is a green-hued spirit with an aniseed (licorice) flavor.

Black Velvet

2 measures Guinness | Champagne, to top

Pour Guinness into a highball glass, then top with Champagne.

Apple Cider Slider

1 measure Morgan's Spiced Rum
1 measure apple schnapps
½ measure cinnamon schnapps

1 dash lemonade
1 apple wedge, to garnish

Shake the rum and both types of
schnapps with ice and strain into
a chilled martini glass. Add a
dash of chilled lemonade, stir,
and garnish with a lemon twist.

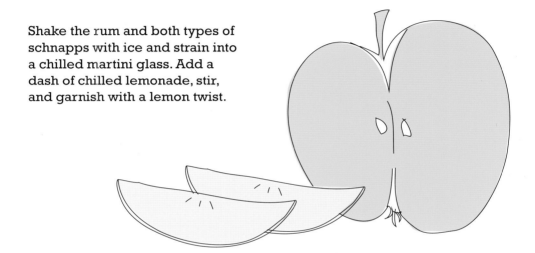

Amaretto Sour

2 measures amaretto
1 measure freshly squeezed
lemon juice

1 dash sugar syrup
1 egg white (see page 69)
4 drops Angostura bitters

Shake all of the ingredients with ice and strain into an ice-filled
old-fashioned glass.

Angel Face

1 measure apricot brandy | **1 measure apple brandy**
1 measure gin | **1 lemon twist, to garnish**

Shake the ingredients with ice and strain into a chilled martini glass.
Garnish with a lemon twist.

Purple Turtle

½ **measure tequila** | ½ **measure sloe gin**
½ **measure blue curaçao** |

Shake all of the ingredients
briefly with ice and strain into
a chilled shot glass.

Red Heat

½ **measure vodka** | ½ **measure Jägermeister**
½ **measure peach schnapps** | 1 dash cranberry juice

Shake all of the ingredients
briefly with ice and strain into
a shot glass.

Tally ho! Jägermeister is a dark brown, bitter-tasting herbal liqueur
made in West Germany and contains a blend of over fifty herbs, fruits,
and spices. If you're drinking this in a shot glass, always ensure it's
nicely chilled first.

Loch Almond

1½ measures amaretto | ginger ale, to top
1½ measures Scotch whisky | 1 amaretti biscuit, to garnish

Build the ingredients over ice in a highball glass. Stir and float the biscuit as the garnish.

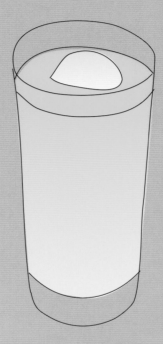

Passion

½ measure cherry brandy | 1½ measures cranberry juice
½ measure bourbon | ½ measure coconut cream (see
½ measure Passoã (passion | page 76)
fruit liqueur) | 2 cocktail cherries, to garnish

Shake all of the ingredients with ice and double strain into a chilled martini glass. Garnish with cherries on a swizzle stick.

Midnight Rambler

2 measures Frangelico
(hazelnut liqueur)

2 measures Bailey's Irish Cream

Pour both ingredients over crushed ice in an old-fashioned glass, and serve with short straws. A wonderful night-cap.

Greek Lightning

½ measure ouzo
½ measure vodka

½ measure Chambord (black raspberry liqueur)

Shake all of the ingredients together and strain into a shot glass. Best served for more than one person.

Green Hornet

½ measure **Pisang Ambon** | 1 tiny dash absinthe
(banana liqueur) | 1 dash lime cordial
½ **measure vodka**

Shake all of the ingredients very briefly with ice and double strain into a chilled shot glass.

China White

½ **measure Bailey's Irish Cream** | ½ **measure white crème de cacao**
½ **measure chilled vodka** | **(chocolate-flavored liqueur)**

Pour all of the ingredients into a shaker, shake very briefly with ice, and strain into a shot glass.

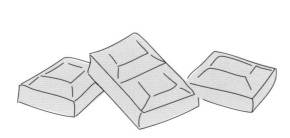

Butterflirt

½ measure butterscotch schnapps
½ measure Bailey's Irish Cream

½ measure chilled Absolut Vanilla
(vanilla-flavored vodka)

In a shot glass layer the
ingredients in the following
order: schnapps, Bailey's, vodka.
Then down in one.

Flatliner

½ measure sambuca
4 drops Tabasco sauce

½ measure gold tequila

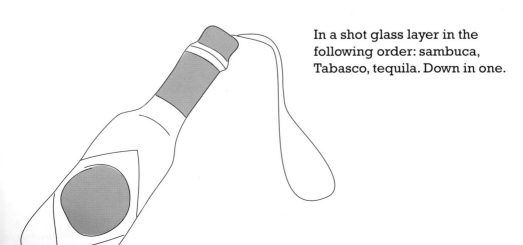

In a shot glass layer in the
following order: sambuca,
Tabasco, tequila. Down in one.

Cowgirl

1 measure chilled peach schnapps
½ measure Bailey's Irish Cream

1 ripe peach wedge

Layer the Bailey's over the schnapps and serve with a wedge of peach to be eaten after the shot.

Indulgence

½ measure amaretto
½ measure dark crème de cacao (chocolate-flavored liqueur)

½ measure Amarula Cream Liqueur

Layer in a shot glass in the order given above (cream at the top).

Rambler

| 1 lime wedge | 1 dash Frangelico |
| 1 measure gold rum | 1 dash strawberry syrup |

Squeeze the lime wedge into a cocktail shaker, then add the three liquid ingredients. Shake briefly with ice and double strain into a chilled shot glass.

Tribbble

| ½ measure butterscotch schnapps | ½ measure Bailey's Irish Cream |
| ½ measure crème de bananes | |

Layer the ingredients in the order given above, with the Bailey's on top.

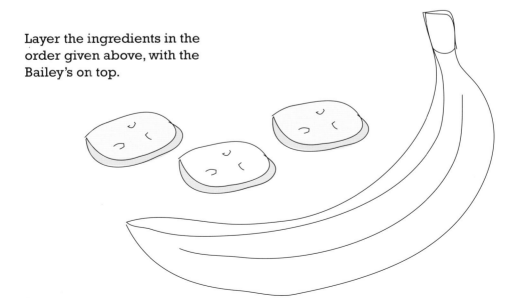

pure & simple

None of the cocktails featured in this section contain alcohol, however, they are a great pick me up if you drank too much alcohol the night before! They are also great as an alternative to alcohol at parties. Packed full of vitamins and minerals, these cocktails taste divine and will rejuvenate and refresh the body and mind. For many of these drinks, a juicer will be required, as the majority of the recipes contain fresh fruit, vegetables, and herbs. It's worth investing in one as fresh fruit juices generally taste much better in cocktails than concentrated juices.

St. Clements

4 measures freshly squeezed
orange juice
4 measures bitter lemon

orange and lemon slices,
to garnish

Pour the ingredients over ice in a highball glass, stir thoroughly, garnish with the orange and lemon slices, and serve with straws.

Virgin Mary

2 dashes Tabasco sauce
4 dashes Worcestershire sauce
celery salt and black pepper

1 dash freshly squeezed lime juice
8 measures tomato juice
1 stick of celery, to garnish

Shake all of the ingredients briefly with ice and strain over ice into a highball glass. Garnish with a stick of celery and serve with straws.

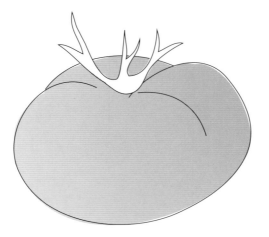

Designer Fuel

½ **ripe mango**
3 strawberries
6 blueberries
1 dash freshly squeezed lime juice

2 measures cranberry juice
4 measures Red Bull (energy drink)
1 split strawberry, to garnish

Blend all of the ingredients with a scoop of crushed ice on high-speed. Serve in a highball glass with straws and garnish with a split strawberry on the rim.

Mango delight To remove the flesh from a mango, run a knife down either side of the seed to remove the two "cheeks." Now run the rim of a wine glass around the inside of the skin, and the flesh will be left on the inside of the glass. You see, there's a trick for everything!

Lemon, Lime & Bitters

1 measure freshly squeezed lime juice
½ measure lime cordial

4 drops Angostura bitters
lemonade, to top
lime wedges, to garnish

Build the first three ingredients over ice in a highball glass. Stir well and top with lemonade. Stir again and garnish with lime wedges.

Loose Juice

2 measures freshly squeezed orange juice
2 measures pineapple juice
2 measures guava juice

2 measures cranberry juice
1 dash passion fruit syrup
1 dash freshly squeezed lime juice
orange slices, to garnish

Shake all of the liquid ingredients with ice and strain over ice into a large highball glass. Garnish with orange slices and serve with straws.

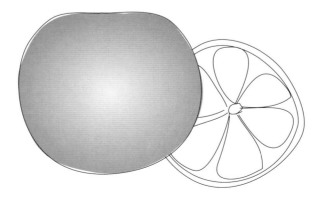

Passion Smash

1 passion fruit
1 dash passion fruit syrup
½ measure freshly squeezed lime juice

2 measures cranberry juice
Red Bull (energy drink), to top
lime wedges, to garnish

Scrape the flesh of the passion fruit into a highball glass (without ice), then add the syrup, lime juice, and cranberry juice. Fill the glass with ice and transfer the contents to a shaker. Shake briefly and return to the highball glass, unstrained. Charge with Red Bull, stir, and garnish with lime wedges.

Seeing red The delicious energy drink, Red Bull, is based on a south-east Asian recipe containing caffeine (less than a cup of regular filter coffee), taurine, and glucuronolactone. It is proven to stimulate the body and mind.

Kiwi & Banana Smoothie

1 kiwi fruit	4 measures milk
½ banana	kiwi slices, to garnish
½ measure vanilla syrup	

Blend all of the liquid ingredients with a small scoop of ice and pour into a highball glass. Garnish with kiwi slices and serve with straws.

Bananarama

½ banana	2 measures Red Bull (energy drink)
2 measures guava juice	lemon slices, to garnish
½ measure freshly squeezed lemon juice	

Blend the liquid ingredients with a small scoop of ice and pour into a highball glass. Garnish with lemon slices and serve with straws.

Go bananas! Do not store your bananas in the fridge. Although it won't affect the flesh, the skin will turn brown and look rather unattractive.

Pineapple & Mint Affair

6 mint leaves
6 chunks fresh pineapple
1 dash sugar syrup
2 measures pineapple juice

1 dash freshly squeezed
lemon juice
soda water, to top
pineapple strips, to garnish

Muddle mint and pineapple chunks with the sugar syrup in the base of a highball glass. Fill the glass with crushed ice and add the juices. Stir, charge with soda water, and garnish with pineapple strips. Serve with large straws.

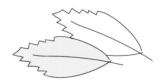

Virginity

4 measures cranberry juice
1 dash black currant cordial
½ measure freshly squeezed
lemon juice

3 measures freshly pressed
apple juice
5 chunks watermelon, to garnish

Blend all of the ingredients with a small scoop of crushed ice and serve in a highball glass with straws. Garnish with whole chunks of fresh watermelon.

Boost Juice

¼ **watermelon** | **orange wedges, to garnish**
2 oranges |

Remove the flesh from the watermelon and peel the oranges. Juice these and then briefly shake with ice. Transfer unstrained into a large highball glass and garnish with wedges of orange. Serve with straws.

Mint Zing

1-inch cucumber slice, roughly | **4 measures freshly pressed**
chopped | **apple juice**
6 mint leaves | **1 mint sprig, to garnish**
2 lime wedges |

Muddle the cucumber, mint leaves, and lime in the base of a shaker. Add the apple juice and shake (without ice). Fill a highball glass with crushed ice and strain the mixture over it. Garnish with a mint sprig and serve with straws.

Cool as a cucumber The cucumber doesn't just taste good. It's also great for flushing out those polluted kidneys.

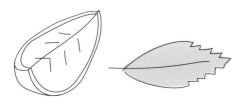

Green Peace

2 carrots | ¾ cup lettuce leaves
1 celery stalk | 2 teaspoons parsley, chopped
½ cup fresh spinach | parsley sprigs, to garnish

Run all of the ingredients through a juicer and then blend the juice with a small scoop of crushed ice. Garnish with parsley sprigs and serve with wide bore straws.

Brushing up The humble toothbrush isn't there just for your teeth, you know! Buy an extra toothbrush for cleaning your juicer. Any residue left on a juicer encourages bacterial growth. After use, wash all parts in warm soapy water and scrub stains with a one part vinegar: two parts water solution.

Free Spirit

4 measures cranberry juice
½ watermelon
8 raspberries

½ measure freshly squeezed
lime juice
lime wedges, to garnish

Blend all of the ingredients with a small scoop of crushed ice and pour into a highball glass. Garnish with lime wedges and serve with straws.

Famous 5

1 tomato
½ cucumber
1 carrot
½ green bell pepper

½ cup fresh spinach
celery salt and freshly ground
black pepper, to taste
cucumber strips, to garnish

Juice the first five ingredients and then shake with the seasoning and ice. Strain over ice into a large highball glass and garnish with strips of cucumber.

Spin City Take your fruit for a spin with the centrifugal juicer. This is the best for juicing fruit and vegetables, other then citrus fruit. It feeds the item through a spinning grater and then separates the pulp from the juice by centrifugal force. Flesh is left in the machine while juice runs out.

Pear Style

1 pear
3 ripe plums
1 stick celery
4 measures freshly pressed
apple juice

1 dash freshly squeezed
lemon juice
pear slices, to garnish

Juice the pear, plums, and celery,
and shake with the apple, lemon,
and ice. Strain into a large
highball glass over ice and
garnish with slices of pear.

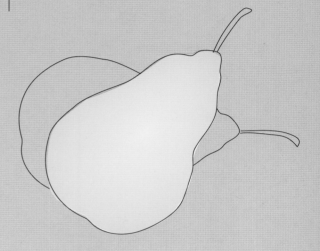

Lush

1 cup unflavored yogurt
1 dash freshly squeezed lime juice
2 measures cranberry juice
4 mint leaves

4 strawberries
½ watermelon
1 split strawberry, to garnish

Blend all of the ingredients
(except the garnish) with a small
scoop of crushed ice and pour
into a large highball glass.
Garnish with the split strawberry
and serve with straws.

Monday Flavors

2 measures freshly squeezed orange juice	1-inch cube of ginger root, chopped
1 small beet	1 carrot

Juice the beet together with the ginger and carrot. Pour into a blender with the orange juice and a small scoop of crushed ice. Blend on high-speed and pour into a highball glass. Serve with straws.

Thyme Out

4 mint leaves	½ measure freshly squeezed lemon juice
1 cup fresh pineapple	
1 sprig thyme	pineapple strips, to garnish

Blend all of the ingredients without ice on high-speed until herbs are well broken down. Strain this mixture over crushed ice in a highball and garnish with pineapple strips. Serve with straws.

Health Freak

½ cup cucumber | 5 radishes
1 small potato | cucumber strips, to garnish
2 carrots |

Juice the first four ingredients, then briefly shake with ice and strain into an ice-filled old-fashioned glass. Garnish with strips of cucumber and serve with straws.

Bora Bora Brew

4 measures pineapple juice | ginger ale, to top
1 dash grenadine | lime wedges, to garnish

Build the ingredients over ice and stir before serving. Garnish with lime wedges.

Swindon Cooler

6 measures freshly squeezed pink grapefruit juice
2 measures lychee juice

1 dash sugar syrup
pink grapefruit wedge, to garnish

Shake the juices and sugar syrup together briefly with ice and strain over ice in a highball glass. Garnish with a wedge of pink grapefruit.

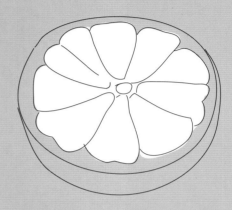

Berry Blush

6 blueberries
3 blackberries
2 teaspoons orgeat syrup (almond syrup)

4 measures freshly squeezed pink grapefruit juice
1 blackberry, to garnish

Muddle the berries and syrup in the base of a highball glass then fill the glass with crushed ice. Top with grapefruit juice and stir. Garnish with a blackberry and serve with straws.

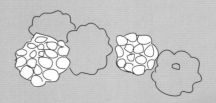

Luxury Iced Tea

½ measure peach juice
½ measure freshly squeezed orange juice
1 dash freshly squeezed lemon juice

1 dash sugar syrup
3 measures cold English Breakfast tea
3 measures cold Earl Grey tea
1 mint sprig, to garnish

Shake all of the ingredients together with ice and strain into a large martini glass over ice. Garnish with a mint sprig and serve with straws. This cocktail is best made in batches and kept refrigerated.

Cocktail Know-How

Every cocktail genius needs to know certain essential information. There is terminology that you should at least be familiar with, and lots of tips on garnishes and equipment that will make you look like the experienced bartender that you aspire to be! A lot of these tips are scattered throughout the chapters but we thought it would be a good idea to compile all of the essential information here in an at-a-glance guide to mixing drinks.

Terminology

BUILDING: this simply means to mix the drink directly in the serving glass. Fill the chosen glass with ice and add each ingredient straight to the glass. Stir before serving.

CHILLING: drink recipes often call for the serving glass to be chilled. To chill a glass simply put the glass in the freezer or refrigerator in advance of preparing the drinks. If this is not possible, place the glass on the counter, fill it with ice, and pour water over the top. When the drink is mixed and ready to be poured, discard the ice and water and pour the cocktail into the chilled glass. Some drinks also call for the liquid ingredients to be chilled or frozen. Spirits such as vodka change viscosity if placed in the freezer for a time and so can give a very different texture to a drink.

CRUSHING ICE: fill a clean tea towel with cubed ice and bash it with a rolling pin to produce perfect crushed ice. Alternatively, you can crush ice in a shaker using a muddle, or pestle.

DOUBLE STRAINING: this is the process by which bits of fruit and flecks of ice are removed from a drink by pouring the cocktail from the shaker through its strainer and then through a tea strainer.

DUSTING: this is where you are instructed to dust an ingredient such as cocoa powder, ground cinnamon or ground nutmeg over the surface of the drink.

FLAVORED SYRUPS: use a batch of homemade sugar syrup as a base and infuse it with your chosen flavor similarly to infusing vodka (see below). Keep the infused syrup refrigerated and keep an eye on it as it will have a very short shelf life depending on what flavor you have used to infuse it.

FLAVORED VODKA: vodka is now available to buy in a wide range of different flavors, but why not have a go at making your own unique vodka at home. Prepare your chosen flavor (fruit, spice, herb etc.) and place it in a bottle of vodka. Seal the bottle and rotate it every two days for two weeks. Filter the infused liquid through coffee filter paper to remove any traces of the fruit, herb, or spice.

FLOATING: to float cream on the surface of a drink, whip the cream so that it still has a liquid quality but is thicker than pouring cream. Stir the drink to create a whirlpool effect and pour the cream over a spoon which is in contact with the drink's surface.

FRUIT PURÉES: Chop the chosen fruit into small pieces and process (without ice) in a blender on a high speed. You may want to adjust the sweetness using some sugar syrup. You may also need to strain the purée before use to get rid of any pips, seeds or small lumps of fruit. A wide selection of purées are available from specialist suppliers.

GLASS HEATING: if you are warming a balloon glass in which to serve brandy, you should always place a metal spoon in the glass before adding boiling water. This will help to disperse the heat and prevent the glass from cracking.

LAYERING (OR POUSSE CAFÉ): this technique will allow you to make a drink where each new ingredient sits in a separate layer on top of each other. It really depends on the density of the liquid and most recipes will instruct you in which order to pour the drinks so that they sit successfully in layers. A general rule to follow is that the higher the alcohol content the lighter the liquid, which will therefore float over less alcoholic liquids.

MUDDLING: this is the process by which a fruit or herb is crushed to release its flavors using a blunt-ended instrument, a muddle, which is similar to a pestle.

SALTING: rub a wedge of lemon or lime around the rim of a glass. Hold the glass upside down and dip the outer rim of the glass into a shallow dish of salt. Twist the glass gently in the salt to ensure the rim is evenly and sufficiently covered.

SHAKING: this is the most fundamental and important mixing technique. Place all ingredients in a shaker and shake!

SUGAR SYRUP: the simplest way to make a homemade sugar syrup is to pour 2 measures of caster sugar into 1 measure of boiling water and stir to dissolve. Leave refrigerated to cool, and remember that it has quite a short shelf life, and should be used within 4 days.

Garnishes

BERRY KEBABS: make mini kebabs on cocktail sticks using a selection of fruit.

CARAMELIZED FRUIT WEDGES: to caramelize a wedge of fruit for use as a sweet garnish, sprinkle the surface of the fruit with fine, powdered sugar and glaze it briefly with a hand-held domestic blow torch until the sugar has melted and slightly browned.

CHILLI CURL: slice the bottom end of the chilli with a sharp knife five or six times, to leave it in little strands at the end of the chilli. Then, submerge this in water for 2 hours—this will cause the strands to curl outwards leaving you with a fantastic looking chilli curl to spice up any cocktail!

CINNAMON FLAME: sprinkle ground cinnamon through a flame to achieve a crackling, sparkly effect which will impart a wonderful flavour to your drink and looks great too!

CITRUS TWISTS: this is a common garnish for fruity drinks as the flavorful oils from the citrus fruit are released into the drink as you drop it in at the last minute. Cut a small disc of skin from any citrus fruit and remove any pith. Pinching the disc skin-side out, squeeze it firmly so that the zest oils are released over the drink and then drop it into the glass.

CITRUS FRUIT OR VANILLA SPIRAL: this pretty garnish can be made using either a strip of citrus fruit peel or a vanilla pod. Wrap the peel or pod around a straw and hold it in place for a few moments. Release it from the straw and it should stay in a spiral shape.

FLAMED ORANGE TWIST: prepare the "twist" in the same way as above for the citrus twist, but leaving a little pith on the inside of the disc. When you pinch the disc to release the oils do this over the drink and also over a flame. The oil will ignite to give you an impressive flare with a fantastic aroma.

FRUIT SHAPES: most fruits can be cut into a multitude of different shapes to make interesting garnishes—try wedges, wheels, slices or slithers or something altogether more interesting.

SPLIT STRAWBERRY: simply make an incision down the length of a strawberry, being careful not to cut all the way through. Open the strawberry and sit both sides on the edge of the glass.

Essential Equipment

BAR SPOON: this spoon has a long handle (about 10 inches/25cm), with an oval or teardrop-shaped bowl. You will see that it is used as a measurement in some of the recipes—if you don't have one you can use a teaspoon to measure as an alternative. The best ones have a twisted stem and a flat end to prevent slipping.

COCKTAIL STICKS/SWIZZLE STICKS: these are invaluable for creating exciting garnishes—experiment with all sorts of fruit and other classic garnishes.

CORKSCREW: you won't be opening any bottles of wine without it!

ICE BUCKET: keep your ice handy with one of these on your home bar.

JIGGER: useful for measuring spirits accurately.

JUICER: freshly squeezed citrus juices make all the difference to a well-mixed and deliciously-flavored drink.

MUDDLER: similar to a pestle, this is used to "muddle" ingredients together in a shaker or glass.

PARING KNIFE: a small, sharp knife, useful for chopping fruit.

PITCHER: this is invaluable for making large quantities of punch or cocktails to serve to groups.

SHAKER: no cocktail genius should be without one! Many drinks require shaking—there are a range of designs available so you can be as traditional or as wacky as you want.

STRAINER: a Hawthorne strainer is most commonly-used in bars

TEA-STRAINER: required when 'double-straining.'

Glassware

BOSTON: a tall, slightly conical glass

BRANDY BALLOON/SNIFTER: a short-stemmed glass with quite a large balloon-shaped bowl. Designed to let the hand warm the drink while the curved sides wafts the aroma upwards.

HIGHBALL/COLLINS: can be used for most tall, long drinks.

OLD-FASHIONED/ROCKS: primarily used for shots of alcohol over ice and some smaller mixed drinks.

SHOT: for single shot drinks made to be drank in one gulp

MARTINI: the traditional cocktail glass with a long stem and a wide brim to disperse the wonderful aroma of the cocktail. Always chill before use.

CHAMPAGNE FLUTE: the tall sides and small surface area allow the bubbles and bouquet of champagne to last longer.

CHAMPAGNE SAUCER: this is another glass (rarely used nowadays) used for serving Champagne, though the wide surface area of the glass allows bubbles to escape faster.

COUPETTE: similar to a Champagne saucer, but a coupette has a deep central 'pocket' in the stem. Traditionally used for serving Margaritas.

SLING: a tall and often stemmed glass similar to a Collins glass, also known as a Catalina glass.

TODDY: a short, heatproof glass used to serve hot drinks.

Index

Special thanks to:

Jack, Charles and Mikey who started it all.

London's underpaid bar-tending workforce—for making and keeping it the world's bar capital. Keep exceeding expectation.

Family, friends and foes for inspiration to create and name my cocktails.

All the intoxicologists who unwittingly contributed recipes.

Sarah Shoo, for all your help, support and head pats.

The G's—much love.

Finally, Abi, thanks for all your patience and belief.